THE FATHER DAUGHTER TALK

R. C. BLAKES, JR.

THE FATHER-DAUGHTER TALK

Copyright 2014 by R. C. Blakes, Jr.

ISBN: 978-1-939779-19-9 (Paperback Edition)
ISBN: 978-1-939779-20-5 (EPUB Edition)

Published by

LIFEBRIDGE
BOOKS
P.O. Box 49428
Charlotte, NC 28277

DEDICATION

This book is dedicated to my wife, Lisa. I grew into a man under the security of your unconditional love. Thank you for always covering my flaws and seeing my potential.

I also dedicate this to my three daughters, Vernitra, Angel, and Rachel, as well as my two nieces Janae and Sariah. At the publishing of this book Rachel, you are a teen on your way into womanhood and college life. Always remember your worth. Never compromise or accept less than you deserve. Remember our talks. As for Vernitra and Angel, I am so proud of the women you are and are yet becoming. Thank you for being the testing ground of all that I have been empowered to teach other women today relative to this subject. To Janae and Sariah, never forget that you are queens in the eyes of your father and your uncle.

This is also dedicated to all of my daughters across the nation. My prayer is to always be a spiritual father of whom you may be proud.

Finally, to my son R. C. Blakes, III. Strive to be better than your Dad. You were born to change the world.

CONTENTS

FOREWORD

by Rachel Blakes

One day I was awaiting service in my hair salon, and I overheard what sounded like some women gossiping, not an irregularity for the setting, so I deemed it irrelevant to me. However, as the conversation continued, the content sparked a feeling of familiarity, as though I were sitting at my dinner table, or riding in the car from school. I continued to listen as one of the women raved about a man speaking at her church and I picked up on the statement: "If you line 10 men up, 9 of them are lying to you."

I knew immediately who this mystery speaker was. He was no mystery to me; he was my father.

This statement was one I had heard and memorized since I could talk—you know; the kind of thing a father says before you go to a dance, or when he first lets you visit the mall alone.

I let the conversation go on a little while longer before I whispered to my hairdresser "I think they're talking about my dad," but I insisted she say nothing. I just smiled and let them continue.

It was then that I knew all the traveling, the long nights and early mornings were worth it. Being able to see all of the hard work come to fruition assured me that his message, *The Father-Daughter Talk,* was one the world desperately needed to hear.

I strongly encourage women, young women and girls alike, to partake in the knowledge that is imparted to us through this book. You will not be disappointed.

– Rachel C. Blakes
(written as a Junior at Second Baptist School Houston, Texas)

INTRODUCTION

Allow me to start with a confession: I HAVE BEEN A WOMANIZER.

Please don't judge me just yet. Womanizing is a deceptive instinct that young men begin to realize, even when they are unaware they are manifesting it. There is a predisposition in the nature of a young pubescent male that drives him instinctively towards sexualization.

This tendency is derived from a male hormone called testosterone which produces an attitude called *machismo*. Merriam-Webster defines the term as an exhilarating sense of power and strength. For the young male there is nothing that expresses this power or demonstrates his innate virility more than sex.

Machismo has a genetic root and is also socially reinforced by cultures that celebrate the reckless sexual expression of men. As a consequence, the young heterosexual man learns to lie, deceive, act and manipulate young women to fulfill this insatiable sexual desire.

These, and other tactics, have been employed by males for generations to place unsuspecting women into positions of sexual vulnerability. These tricks are learned from the examples of the older generation of men in the male's circle, television, music, and social interaction with other contemporary men.

It is from this vantage point that I approach the subject at hand. *The Father-Daughter Talk* is a candid discussion about the psyche and thought process of men, in general, who will do anything to take advantage of an unsuspecting female. It is an in-your-face reality check for twenty-first century women who hold to early twentieth-century ideals that no longer exist for most.

What you are about to read is a heartfelt letter a father would write to his daughters from a death bed. It is the father's instruction manual of womanhood and how to survive and thrive in a world full of obstacles and predators.

Now, to put you at ease, allow me to also clarify, *I am no longer a womanizer.* That was a lifetime ago.

MY AWAKENING

Like most red blooded ego-driven men, I found a sense of godless and depraved pleasure in my conquests of the opposite sex. However, from a more matured platform, I now understand the responsibility I have to enlighten the many women who know me as a pastor, counselor, motivator, mentor, and friend. On a more profound level, I serve as a husband and father.

My greatest motivation comes from the fact that I am the father of three daughters and uncle to two nieces.

One day I had an awakening; I realized that my own daughters and nieces were coming of age. It is not a good feeling for a man to ask himself the question, "Would I want my girls to have a man like me?" and then hear himself respond with a resounding, "NO!"

From that point, I began to look at matters from a different perspective. My thinking shifted to the impact my actions had on the women I once deceived. I was transformed from the predator to the protector as I began to ponder how I could communicate to my girls the games men play.

As a father, a man should naturally lend his thought process to the reality that every woman is somebody's daughter, mother, wife, sister, or friend. When a man matures to view every woman as such, it breeds a natural respect for womankind.

It was during this same season in my life the Lord revolutionized my thinking and delivered me from a lifetime of sexual irresponsibility. God made me a devoted husband and father. As a result, I realized that one of my passions is to empower women to succeed in life, even against the odds. The same intent I have towards my biological and spiritual daughters is the concern and desire I have for all women worldwide.

Being a father and pastor, I am hyper-sensitive to the plight of all of my daughters. Almost on a weekly basis, I am left to deal with women who have been broken by the misdealings of immature and insensitive men. Women are used sexually, and emotionally abused as their expectations of the opposite sex rarely tend to be what they really experience.

Why are women so susceptible to the trickery and deceits of less intelligent men? In other words, how are smart women tricked by dumb men?

PhD women are being mastered by GED men. Wow! How?

Why don't they know better than to fall for every lie? Why do women invest themselves into men who make no investment back? I pondered these questions and came to one primary answer: *nobody is teaching the women the games that men play!*

As a society, we are releasing our innocent daughters into a world that will eat them alive, and we are failing to bring them up to speed concerning the realities they will face. This breakdown has occurred because of a shaky father-daughter dynamic.

Socially, we are conditioned to believe that girls need mothers exclusively, while sons need fathers exclusively. This is most untrue.

According to behavioral practitioner Robin Webster:

> As a Licensed Professional Counselor (LPC) who is also Nationally Certified to Counsel (NCC), I have had the opportunity to witness first hand some of the emotional and psychological effects of young girls and women who have been reared in fatherless homes.
>
> In today's society, where single mother households have become the norm with one too many girls and women having to grow up without positive, active, and present fathers in their lives, it is undeniable that the father's absence has left some of our daughters at an unmerited emotional and psychological deficit. This deficit has unfortunately led to many unanswered questions and emotional voids that have led and continue to lead to unhealthy behaviors.

The end result in far too many cases are girls who have become women wrestling with low self esteem, depression, issues of self worth, body image, lack of self-confidence, as well as trust and boundary issues and so on.

The one thing that is often overlooked in the dialogue regarding the importance of fathers is the severe impact that is made on a young woman who has had no real father figure in her life. The father-daughter dynamic is a major piece of the puzzle in raising healthy and whole young women.

ONE WOMAN'S JOURNEY

Allow me to share the story of an anonymous African-American Puerto-Rican female:

Although my father and I have never enjoyed a close relationship, I am and have always been a daddy's girl. Not having him participate in my life has been extremely painful and has often left me feeling inadequate.

My father was the first man I ever loved and the first man to repeatedly break my heart. We both have very different ideas about what being a father means. He views it solely as a financial provider and feels that he met his obligation by paying child support. I, on the other hand, envision a man who not only provides financially, but gives spiritual, emotional, and physical support as well.

Growing up, I was captivated by moments when I saw little girls interacting with their fathers. Whether it was a father expressing his love or disciplining his daughter, it was an experience and a relationship that I longed for. Pure observation just wasn't enough...I wanted my daddy!

There was a point in my life when I was on a mission to win my father over by achieving and excelling in everything I did. My thinking was that if I behaved appropriately and excelled in school, he would have reason to be proud and desire to be in my life. I executed my strategy and did exceptionally well in my studies. I approached every opportunity with fervor. I rarely got into trouble and avoided anything that would bring my father shame. The last thing I wanted to do was give him reason to reject me anymore than he already had.

Unfortunately, my hopes for our father-daughter relationship never came to fruition and resulted in constant disappointment, as my dad never took any interest in me, good or bad.

After more than two decades of rejection, I've accepted my father's choice to opt out of my life. To date, I am dealing with the aftermath of his rebuff and trying to remedy the hurt, frustration, and resentment that is intensified when I reflect on the failed relationship.

In rejecting me, my father in essence rejected himself. He pushed me away, but I ended up in arms that have held me close and hands that have promised to never forsake me. I found myself in the safeguard of my heavenly Father. He is the Creator of all things, and unlike my earthly father, He takes pride in His creation and loves with a love incomprehensible to man.

My story is unfinished, and I continue to write because the chapter on me and my earthly father is incomplete. Even harboring feelings of disgust, anger, resentment, and overall disappointment, there is still a little girl within me who yearns for HER daddy and awaits the father-daughter talk. I don't believe that the desire will ever leave, and so far, it has only subsided.

I have encountered hundreds of real life examples of young and older women who are broken emotionally because their fathers were not there for them. As we observe this social climate and the absence of filters or boundaries in many women today, we must ask the question: *where were the fathers?*

When the male parent is absent it is as emotionally tragic for the young girl as it would be physically perilous to leave a toddler alone on a busy street. She will make choices that are self destructive while trying to navigate a world she has not been adequately prepared for.

> *Much of the sexually extroverted behavior that young women display today is their futile attempt to fill a void. It's an empty vacuum that Daddy should have filled.*

According to Dr. Ken Canfield, founder of the National Center for Fathering, "When a father abandons a relationship with his daughter, she can become frozen in time, relationally, with the opposite sex. A 50-year-old woman may look like

17

an adult on the outside, but on the inside she is still working on issues that should have been attended to by a healthy, engaged father."

According to the research, girls who lack a healthy relationship with their father will look for other ways to contribute to their development when it comes to relating to men.

As Dr. Canfield explains, "When you are frozen relationally, it is difficult to know your place and how to develop a healthy relationship because you are working from a point of need instead of working out of a position of co-equal." He adds, "There is a void in her life and the search to fill that void prompts her to take risks in relationships which usually result in some really poor choices."

THE FIRST EXAMPLE

A woman may gain some perspective, relative to what a real worthy man should encompass, from the first man, Adam, written about in Genesis. Actually, from Adam we also get a glimpse of how a father should nurture his daughters.

The first woman found her original makeup in Adam. He was the physical source of Eve.

18

According to Scripture, *"The Lord God caused a deep sleep to fall upon Adam, and he slept: and he took one of his ribs, and closed up the flesh instead thereof; and the rib, which the Lord God had taken from man, made he a woman, and brought her unto the man. And Adam said, This is now bone of my bones, and flesh of my flesh: she shall be called Woman, because she was taken out of Man"* (Genesis 2:21-23).

Adam served as a type of father to Eve and is a prototype of what young women need from a male parent.

Of course, Adam did not father Eve in a sexual fashion, but, in principle, he played the same role in her existence that natural fathers play in the lives of their daughters. He was the DNA source of her makeup. Beyond the physical contribution, Adam had a major role in demonstrating the intangible investments a father should make into the life of his daughters.

There are three important aspects to this story:

First: Adam fathered Eve out of selflessness.

The first man actually had to give of himself (one of his ribs) for Eve to exist. Fathering, in general, must be a selfless endeavor. A true parent must be willing to die for his children. A young girl may develop the confidence to face the world to

19

the extent that she is raised in a secure environment where her father is always there for her, no
matter what the cost.

Second: Adam fathered Eve from a place of security.

The rib cage is the major portion of the chest
cavity. This cavity represents a place of security
and safety. The bosom is where a parent nurtures
a young child. So the first woman, Eve, came from
the place of protection. Her first subliminal
message regarding man was that of safety.

A father must do more in the life of his
daughter than to merely provide financially.
Provision is a primary responsibility, but it is not
the *only* obligation of fathering. Especially in the
life of a daughter, a father must cherish and keep
her close to his bosom.

Third: Adam fathered Eve from a place of sincerity.

Any basic sense of human biology denotes that
the rib cage envelops most of the vital organs, in
particular, *the heart*—which is almost always a
symbol of that which is pure, transparent, and
trustworthy. Eve was taken from a part of Adam
that represents emotional connection and sincerity.

*One of a man's greatest challenges
in rearing daughters is to maintain
the emotional connection.*

To anyone who has parented long enough to raise children to adulthood, it should not be a secret that the child's sense of pride and self-worth are established in the relationship with the parent.

As King Solomon wrote, *"Children's children are the crown of old men; and the glory of children are their fathers"* (Proverbs 17:6). The Message version translates it this way: *"Grandparents are distinguished by grandchildren; children take pride in their parents."*

Recently, in my parental life, I have begun to learn something about my adult children, who happen to be daughters. I always thought that once they were grown, educated, and financially independent, my greatest responsibilities to them would be over. I was sadly mistaken. My adult daughters pulled me on the carpet about their need for me to be emotionally available for them. I had become so carried away with all of my responsibilities that I allowed a gap to develop in our fellowship. They communicated in no uncertain terms that I have more of a fatherly role in their lives now than I did when they were children.

As I write this, my oldest daughter is a school teacher in Texas. She has completed her Masters and has begun work on her Doctorate. Whenever she changes locations, I make a point to visit her new school. When I arrive, it is not uncommon for her to scream down the halls to the other educators, "That's my daddy! That's my daddy!"

She is a mother herself and well advanced in her career, yet she still finds a certain measure of pride in her relationship with me as her father. WOW! This was a welcome revelation for me.

SOMETHING IS MISSING

In the words of an anonymous woman: "A father should understand that a daughter, no matter the age, will ALWAYS NEED HER FATHER. This is especially important when she has grown up predominately with the mother. Under such circumstances, the daughter often feels lost and suffers inadequacies, voids and uncertainties, as if something vital is missing."

It seems that young girls are built with an innate desire to be accepted and admired by a prominent male figure. This longing for such a healthy relationship is not a surprise. God made woman in such a way that she is hyper-sensitive to male influence.

Fallen society provides the clearest proof of this internal longing and deep need in young females to have an intimate bond with a male figure. The prime example is in the fact that young women who, in most cases, did not have a healthy relationship with a father are drawn into prostitution by the influence of a deceptive man who promises to be to them what Daddy should have been: provider, protector, and supporter.

Of course, their pursuits, in that direction, are futile and can ultimately end in heartbreak and more emotional scarring.

> *Practically every intimate*
> *relationship women develop with men*
> *are either an attempt to distance herself from*
> *a negative father, perpetuate the security*
> *of a good father, or she is fishing for*
> *the father she never had.*

It comes as no surprise that womankind is longing for male acceptance and embrace. God made Eve this way. In Scripture we read: *"To the woman, he said, I will greatly multiply thy sorrow and thy conception; in sorrow, thou shalt bring forth children; and thy desire shall be to thy husband, and he shall rule over thee"* (Genesis 3:16).

Notice the phrase, *"thy desire shall be to thy husband."* This speaks of a God-given yearning placed in a woman to please her husband. A typical, heterosexual female finds her greatest joy in pleasing three men, namely: father, husband and son.

Her primary desire is to make the man she is in love with happy. She will work her fingers to the bone to see that he is pleased with her endeavors.

As we have discussed, the interesting dynamic regarding Adam and Eve is that Adam symbolically served as the father of Eve because he was her physical DNA pool, and he was also her husband. This is significant because the Bible promotes the idea that there is a clear consistency between the responsibilities of a loving father and a potential husband in the life of a woman.

Apart from sex, everything a woman finds in a good father should be experienced with a good husband.

For example, the father provides, protects,

empowers, and guides. The husband provides, protects, empowers, and guides. For the woman, essentially the transition to a biblical husband is consistent with a healthy father relationship. This point is important because a woman will make relationship choices, unconsciously, based on what she has received and/or did not receive from her father.

> *When the woman has not had the proper fathering, she takes her social signals from the foremost male perspective to which she is exposed.*

I am frequently left to shake my head at some of the negative choices women make for relationships and overall life decisions. More often than not, when we dig deeper into her background, usually, her father has either been absent physically or is missing emotionally.

Because a woman is built to lean towards the opinions of a dominant male influence, this creates a crisis. She is left to settle for the perspective of the most dominant male images in her particular world.

In today's culture, young people are greatly influenced by what they see on television and in entertainment. This means that a non-existent father may very well be replaced by the leading voices of hip hop or heavy metal. When a father is absent, the world always has counterfeit influences to guide the girl down the wrong path.

Most male perspectives will serve to pervert her rather than empower her.

When a young woman is without the guidance of a loving father, she is inundated with worldly male influences which are designed to mislead, so they might prey on her. This fact is demonstrated in a society filled with young fatherless women and how they interact with each other.

When I was growing up, if a man referred to a woman as a female dog—the "B" word—there was going to be a fight. Today, this fatherless generation of women have so assimilated to the perverted male culture, they use such language as a term of endearment among each other. They are not at all offended when their men refer to them as "bitches." This word is so disrespectful that it even felt weird typing it. Sadly, ours is a generation of young women who have been conditioned with disorder and dysfunction.

When natural fathers are absent, God designates spiritual fathers to subsidize the deficiencies in the daughters.

As I reflect on the condition of daughters today, it awakens a mandate that lies deep in my soul to speak to the pain and to utter words of wisdom to the lack thereof. As a spiritual father, I am commissioned to address, with effectiveness, the issues that we have turned a blind eye to in the lives of our daughters.

On these pages I will discuss what every daughter should hear from her father regarding herself as a person, the general psychology of men, and the games they play. My goal is to break down the game—and also break it up—in order to help close the doors of dysfunction on the anguish that is the consequence of ignorance.

BUCKLE UP "LIL" GIRL!

PART I

THE THINGS EVERY WOMAN SHOULD HEAR FROM A FATHER

CHAPTER 1

YOUR DRESS CODE IS YOUR PERSONAL COMMERCIAL

It was evening and I was reading through some Facebook postings of friends, family, and church members—and there it was. It was a message from a young lady who was visibly attractive and obviously intelligent, based on her use of words.

In spite of the initial positive impression, the posting quickly turned bizarre. As I continued to read, she wrote something that had the undertones of a woman not short of clueless. In her post, she was addressing other women. She said, "Try your brains. Use your articulation and your education. When all else fails, fall back on your booty," as in derriere, "behind," bottom, or buttocks.

I was shocked!

All I could visualize were my daughters and

nieces and how I would feel had they posted something so self-abasing. In essence, her message was: use the promotion of your body to get ahead in this world. Use your bottom to get to the top. Use your sexuality as a success strategy.

Unfortunately, this person had been conditioned to believe that HER FUTURE IS BEHIND HER! Think about it. How sad!

The spirit of that posting seems to be the prevailing mindset of young and even older women today. Many actually feel that they must flaunt themselves as sexual objects to solicit the attention of men. This mindset promotes overt sexuality in the way a woman adorns herself for the world to see. She finds herself exposing more and more of her flesh in an attempt to garner the interest she craves from society, and specifically, men.

Again, this is another sad consequence of the moral deficiency in judgment to which a fatherless generation of women fall victim.

For Christian women, to flaunt their body and sex appeal as the primary message for all to see is most contradictory.

The Bible has very specific standards concerning the dress code of female believers. The Apostle Paul wrote to the young pastor Timothy pertaining to this important topic: *"In like manner also, that women adorn themselves in modest apparel, with shamefacedness and sobriety; not with braided hair, or gold, or pearls, or costly array; but (which becometh women professing godliness) with good works"* (1 Timothy 2:9-10).

The text is really not a detailed document on appropriate feminine attire; rather, it is a principle text highlighting certain values that should be consistent with every Christian culture and time period relative to the woman's approach to her wardrobe and dress.

It is a principle that alters itself from one generation to the next. What was considered modest and acceptable attire in Paul's time won't apply today. What was conservative apparel in the 1960s does not apply in the 21st century. However, the basic tenant of the principle is transferable to every generation.

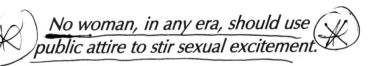

No woman, in any era, should use public attire to stir sexual excitement.

LET YOUR DRESS CODE BE CONSISTENT WITH YOUR MORAL CODE

No self-respecting woman should expose the areas of her body that should be considered private. And no female should dress in a way that society concludes, just by the way she is clothed, that she is provocative and sexually inviting.

The real message is that a Christian woman should not mislead the world to define her as something she is not based on a dress code that sends the wrong message.

When teaching this, I make this point: if a prostitute is working on a street corner and you, another woman, pass by, those looking on should be able to determine the prostitute from you. Today, the dress code has become so liberal that many Christian women are wearing the same exploitive, seductive clothing that common prostitutes are wearing. This should not be!

God calls for each of us to exhibit a personal standard that will be pleasing to Him in everything we do. We belong to God, and our actions and behavior should reflect our sanctification unto Him.

Pause for a moment and read what is recorded in God's Word: *"They have violated my law, and have profaned mine holy things: they have put no difference between the holy and profane, neither have they shewed difference between the unclean and the clean, and have hid their eyes from my Sabbaths, and I am profaned among them"* (Ezekiel 22:26).

The necessity of a woman understanding the

importance of monitoring her image to the world goes beyond Jewish/Christian principles. It is a matter of self-respect. It is appreciation for the struggle that generations of women before them have encountered to be viewed as equals, and it's the overall wisdom of the woman in an over-sexed male-dominated society to promote her more virtuous assets.

> *Never dress to attract attention; dress to project conviction. If you want to be respected for your mind, as a woman, don't promote your "behind."*

For a woman, image is everything! It will determine if your boss will give attention to your brain or your bust line. It will dictate if a man will look inside to see your real worth or just stop on the surface at your sex appeal.

When a female disregards personal boundaries and allows herself to display an image of explicit sexuality through her dress code, she is dismantling all of the work that women have done for generations to fight for equality.

It's been less than one hundred years since women have been respected enough to obtain the right to vote in the United States. It was the suffragette movement in the early twentieth century that fought for these basic rights.

Women, traditionally, have been relegated to two functions in this male controlled society—the bedroom to satisfy the sexual urges of the man, and the kitchen to satisfy his dietary needs. Neither of these functions recognizes nor respects the woman as a thinking being created on a co-equal level.

When females use their dress code to attract sexual attention from men, other than their husbands, they are reconditioning a new generation of men to view them as sexual objects and not social and intellectual contemporaries. This is unfortunate.

The woman has always lived from a pseudo-inferior position which has been perpetuated by insecure men in power. However, it is one thing for someone else to continue your bondage unjustly and quite another when you, the marginalized, actively promote your own social enslavement by willing acts of self destruction.

Lacking limitations in how much she will reveal and how she will sexually present herself publicly, re-enforces all of the lies that men believe about the woman's subservient place in society.

From the beginning of this nation, women have been diminished to a sexual utensil. During

35

American slavery, the black woman with her rounded hips and full figure could not elude the lustful advances of the white slave master. She would be stripped from her husband and children and used at will by her enslaver for sexual exploitation. She had no option. But women today, who have a choice, choose to willingly offer themselves, in the court of public opinion, as nothing more than sexual objects.

Even the white wife of the slave master was used for child bearing and social decoration. She, too, was just a well-kept emotional and psychological slave at the discretion of a perverted male dominant culture.

With all of this history and victory, one would think that modern twenty-first century women would never position themselves as public entertainment for a perverted male society.

When we look at the videos and CD covers, we see how women are selling their honor to the highest bidder.

FIRST IMPRESSIONS ARE LASTING

I've heard from my daughters, "People need to focus on my intellect." This argument sounds great in an ideal world where individuals truly judge by content rather than image. However, in this culture, 99 percent of the time we are judged and defined by what we appear to be at first glance. All of this happens before we utter a word or perform any act.

A man is not built to focus on intellect and inner value first. A man is moved by what he first sees.

As it relates to how a man views and judges a woman, it is clear that far too often he makes his opinions purely based on visual stimulation.

The Bible gives us a hint of how a man is wired. In Genesis, we have the account of Adam's creation. When you pay close attention to the Scripture, it explains how and why men think the way we do: *"And the Lord God formed man of the dust of the ground, and breathed into his nostrils the breath of life; and man became a living soul"* (Genesis 2:7).

Notice, man was created from the dust of the earth—meaning he finds his origin in things tangible and visible. This will prove to be relevant in how the male will embrace the world and life. A man, as a consequence of his base nature, will always have a pull to the things that he experiences visually and tangibly. When a man sees a woman scantily dressed, his mind and focus immediately go to a sexual place.

Many men are misdirected by good women wearing a poor choice of clothing. She is usually much more than she is projecting.

Once a male sees a female as a sexual object, his sense of reasoning is turned off. When a woman awakens a man's sexual imagination, it will be quite difficult for her to reverse the momentum to get him to focus on the more substantive aspects of her mind and character. A wise person will lead with the intellect and character and allow the sexual to naturally find its place sometime later, after a firm foundation has been established.

It is just not smart stewardship of womanhood to flaunt herself publicly. I am a pastor, and I have been disturbed on Sunday mornings watching some of the sisters walk around at offering time in inappropriate outfits they wear to church. Deacons and those present should not be distracted by the skin tight, almost waist-high skirts certain sisters wear. This is God's house, and should be honored accordingly.

38

The Lord gave the woman the ability to captivate the man; however, that power should be reserved for her covenant man (husband).

What women often fail to understand is that they are major stumbling blocks to heterosexual men. A normal guy is addicted to a beautiful woman. Though his addiction may be under control, when she exposes too much or flaunts what she has, it is like pouring cocaine on the pillow of a drug addict. A woman's dress code may either help a man to grow spiritually and socially or test him beyond his ability to withstand.

Here is what the Bible counsels: *"But put ye on the Lord Jesus Christ, and make not provision for the flesh, to fulfil the lusts thereof"* (Romans 13:14).

The text admonishes Christians to behave in a way that does not give the flesh any advantage or life. The argument has been made by some women that they have the right to wear whatever they want to because God is looking on the heart and not the outside. This is true; but, what we wear externally is supposed to be a witness of who we are internally. And even though we have the right to wear what we please, we are still

39

responsible to consider whether our actions are providing a stumbling block for the faith of someone else.

The Apostle Paul wrote: *"For, brethren, ye have been called unto liberty; only use not liberty for an occasion to the flesh, but by love serve one another"* (Galatians 5:13).

He is warning us not to abuse our freedom. We must not act without regard for the impact our choices will make on others.

For a Christian woman, I believe it boils down to the following questions:

- Should I or shouldn't I wear a particular garment?
- Will I be able to effectively witness for Christ to everybody while wearing this clothing?
- Will I be able to reflect Christ in word, deed, and by my presence?

In essence, if you are dressed in an article of clothing that will hinder your light from shining, you should consider wearing something else. Ask, "Will my future husband be able to recognize me as the potential mother of his children in this get-up?"

A woman should always dress like somebody's wife or mother.

I was impressed by the words of Monique R. Henry, who holds a masters degree in public health and is a Health, Environment, and Safety Specialist for a major oil company. She states:

The idea that a woman must dress seductively to be desired and pursued by the opposite sex is false. Women who dress provocatively are not regarded as women of worth, in either the male or female community. In a small, personal and far-from-scientific survey of men, whose opinions I regard as standard, they have stated that there is no serious interest in a relationship with a provocatively dressed woman. Instead, they prefer a woman that dresses modestly and carries herself in an indisputably lady like manner.

In addition to being a deterrent to finding a godly man, dressing provocatively also creates unnecessary obstacles to advancing professionally.

No matter where you are, you are being observed. In some cases your presentation can be a distraction for people who could open doors of great opportunity for you. Someone who God puts in your path may not be able see beyond your external message.

I dress stylish but modestly because you never know what you may be called to do. Countless times I have had opportunities for success and being a modestly dressed person, to represent the company or organization that I worked for, gave me the leg up over my competition.

Oh, that women everywhere would heed this advice. Remember, your dress code is your personal commercial.

What are you advertising?

CHAPTER 2

YOUR VALUE IS NOT DETERMINED BY YOUR RELATIONSHIP WITH A MAN

Do not be emotionally and psychologically incarcerated by the idea that a man absent from your life is a handicap.

Why do women buy into the concept that they are worth less when they don't have a man on their arm or they still carry their maiden name? This negative way of thinking is a product of female slave conditioning.

Some of the greatest women we know, and have known, are single sisters.

The male dominated world promotes the

notion that the ideal for a woman is a good man. As a consequence, the woman lowers her ambitions and ignores her dreams to pursue a relationship with the perfect man as opposed to following the path of a relevant and fulfilling life.

Don't get me wrong. God definitely designed the system for a powerful woman to connect with a powerful man; but that dynamic is not the entirety of the Father's plan, nor is it the primary agenda in God's purpose.

There are a few problems with the philosophy of "all she needs is the ideal man."

First, there is no such thing! Even Adam, the original male creation of God, was not perfect. We know this because the Bible tells us, *"And the Lord God said, It is not good that the man should be alone; I will make him an help meet for him"* (Genesis 2:18).

So the woman was created to HELP the man. The reason he needed assistance is because there were some things that would unravel without support. NO MAN IS PERFECT. God gives a man a wife for the purpose of helping to perfect certain areas of his life.

The next drawback with limiting your value is, as a woman, the man you are in a relationship with may use your passion for marriage as a leash to lead you everywhere but to the altar. When a woman is married to the *idea* of marriage, she is left vulnerable to manipulation on the part of a deceptive, indecisive, and immature male.

Even in the church, the concept that a woman's ideal life is only experienced in the context of marriage is promoted vigorously. People endorse marriage as if it is the ultimate existence. Matrimony is a gift from God if one has the right mate; but just to be married for the sake of marriage is ludicrous. In fact, you are not really a good candidate for marriage until you are totally productive and content being single.

The Apostle Paul addressed this issue with the church at Corinth: *"For I would that all men were even as I myself. But every man hath his proper gift of God, one after this manner, and another after that. I say therefore to the unmarried and widows; It is good for them if they abide even as I"* (1 Corinthians 7:7-8).

Paul told them, "It is better for you to be single as I am." This contradicts the traditional view which states: if you are not married or seriously engaged, especially as a woman, you are somehow deficient.

The apostle explained, *"There is difference also between a wife and a virgin. The unmarried woman careth for the things of the Lord, that she may be holy both in body and in spirit: but she that is married careth for the things of the world, how she may please her husband"* (1 Corinthians 7:34).

Paul explains how it is good to be single because you are not preoccupied with the cares a married person has. When you are single and content, you can devote yourself to God's agenda and your purpose in life.

A woman should be so focused on pleasing God and maximizing her personal potential that she does not have time to concentrate on when she's getting married, how old she's becoming, and how many of her friends are unhappily wed.

When we look at many of the women in the Bible, they were busy self-actualizing when their would-be husbands found them. They were not desperately searching for a man to bring them some fleeting social significance. For instance, Rebekah was discovered by Abraham's servant while she was serving animals water at the well. He eventually brought her back to marry the young heir, Isaac.

Boaz found Ruth gleaning grain in his fields. God brought Eve to Adam. None of these women were in a panic or desperation mode for a man.

If you ever want to attract the love of a real husband, begin by falling in love with yourself.

We get a glimpse at what a healthy single mindset looks like from Adam and Eve. They were single before they were married. They both embraced their individuality before they merged their assets.

When we go back to the creation of Adam and Eve, we see that God made the man first. Then, after he spent some time with God alone, the Creator made Eve. In the process, the Lord put Adam to sleep. This means that God had private time with both Adam and Eve before He ever brought the two together. Individually, they had full lives before joining each other.

Another interesting observation is that we find no hint of Adam asking for Eve or Eve asking for Adam. All indications are that they both found their total sense of joy, purpose, and identity in God before they connected.

A woman today must never get caught in the trap of needing a man on her arm to feel worthwhile.

A REAL QUEEN DOES NOT NECESSARILY NEED A KING TO REIGN

I took a lesson from my flight experiences. Due

to my ministry responsibilities of serving as pastor between two states, there are occasions where I fly on private planes. Sometimes the aircraft has two pilots; while on other trips, there is a single pilot. Regardless of there being one or two at the controls, the plane can always be managed by just one pilot.

Life is a journey. Often we have the luxury of co-pilots; if not, we will still manage the ride and arrive at our intended destination on time.

As a woman, you must have it firmly fixed in your psyche that whatever God put in you will bring you to greatness—with or without a co-pilot.

One of England's most memorable monarchs was Queen Elizabeth I, who was on the throne from 1558 to 1603. She was a spinster queen her entire reign.

Every young woman should know that she has more than enough within herself to make a full contribution to society and the kingdom of God. She must divorce herself from the idea that she is inferior or second rate because she does not yet have a man. You must take a full view of your personal assets and realize that you are enough all by yourself.

Rejoice and say with the psalmist: *"I will praise thee; for I am fearfully and wonderfully made: marvelous are thy works; and that my soul knoweth right well"* (Psalm 139:14).

The term *marvelous* refers to something that is unique, one of a kind. The word literally means "singular" as in a stand-alone value. In other words, we, men and women, must know our worth apart from any relational connection we may make.

Your significance is never lost because of the absence of any relationship and is not solidified because of the acquisition of a relationship. You are always whole and complete as a stand-alone person.

When the young Kate Middleton was being interviewed regarding her upcoming nuptials to Prince William of England, she was asked, "Do you feel lucky to be marrying the Prince?"

She quickly replied, "He's lucky to be marrying me!"

How many women would have been bold enough to say those words? How many would even have enough self-appreciation to actually think that way? Not many.

There is nothing more attractive to an eligible man than a confident, independent and self-assured woman.

One of the things that made the Virtuous

Woman of Proverbs 31 so outstanding was not her husband, but the fact that this individual loved and valued herself, followed her dreams, and lived her life fully. She did not allow herself to be forced into the mode of lost identity because she had a prominent husband. She knew who she was, independent of her spouse.

As it is written: *"She perceiveth that her merchandise is good: her candle goeth not out by night"* (Proverbs 31:18).

When you read the full account of the virtuous woman, she ran businesses, participated in charity, made money, took care of her children, and still blessed her husband. This woman's life was full, with or without a man.

*Sometimes a woman needs
to get a life to get a man.*

Many women with tremendous potential have wasted it by sitting on the sidelines when they should have been in the game. Why idly wait for a man to bring you happiness, success, and acclaim when you are empowered by your heavenly Father to provide these things for yourself? There is great honor in marriage; however, there is nothing more dishonoring to God than to check out of life because your finger wears no wedding ring and your bed is only warmed by one person.

There are some very practical reasons that the modern woman has to rise above yesterday's ideals.

Many years ago, a woman really had a shot at marrying a husband who would totally provide for the family and be committed to her welfare. Today, the economic and social climate of the world does not feed this concept. Employment is not what it once was. The global economy has moved high-paying jobs to other parts of the globe.

The increasing demand on men to have post-graduate degrees also has an impact; because without such credentials a husband will view his ability to provide for and to keep a wife as improbable.

As the capacity to earn has dwindled, so has the man's desire to take the big leap into marriage. Those who do get married are often looking for a woman who is motivated and self-sufficient. The days of the fragile stay-at-home wife who has no skill or trade is long gone.

This is the age of the power couple.

A strong, independent man is searching for a secure, self-sufficient woman who knows her true worth and potential, independent of him.

There are some social realities that also suggest a woman today must recondition her mind regarding a relationship with a man. Some of these realities are the explosion of the gay male population and the rate of incarceration of heterosexual men. All of this further depletes the pool of would-be husbands and boyfriends who could fill the demands of the heterosexual female population. In other words, in many instances, there are not enough men to go around.

THREE THINGS THAT GIVE A WOMAN VALUE

In today's world, a woman must find value and purpose in something greater than cohabitation with a person of the opposite sex. This is solidified in three areas which are independent of any formal union.

1. A woman's worth is found in the realization of her relationship to God.

When a woman knows the Lord personally, there are no limits to her success. Scripture plainly states, *"Favour is deceitful, and beauty is vain: but a woman that feareth the Lord, she shall be praised"* (Proverbs 31:30).

When the Almighty is the foundation of a

woman's existence, she wakes up every morning with the odds in her favor. She has to know that God is enough.

2. A woman's value is tied to her willingness to be fully productive.

Far too many women bury their talents and ignore their gifts simply to settle for a socially acceptable level of mediocrity.

May it be said of you: *"Give her of the fruit of her hands; and let her own works praise her in the gates"* (Proverbs 31:31).

Take great pride in finding and following a daily agenda and purpose.

One of the many things that attracted me to my wife, Lisa, is that she had a purpose to fulfill, and she was defined by something other than simply being my wife.

When a woman is buried in the identity of a man, she has a breakdown when things fail in a relationship.

3. A woman finds worth in her management of money.

Any individual who knows the laws of mastering money will always be honored. A woman that does not buy into the typical mall-crazed mindset will never be enslaved. She will forever be viewed and treated as a queen in the midst of kings.

My advice to younger sisters may make you smile: "Don't work on increasing your bust line. Work on increasing your bottom line through education and personal initiative."

There is power and significance in being a financially independent woman.

CHAPTER 3

NEVER LAY YOUR BODY DOWN FOR A MAN WHO HAS NOT LAID DOWN HIS LIFE FOR YOU

It strikes me as odd and even perplexing that in every generation, women are becoming easier targets for the sexual exploitation of predators. I am not just referring to a pedophile or rapist—it includes men who want to use a woman for her body as a sexual object.

The man whose only intention is to satisfy a physical function with an insecure or misguided young woman who does not know her worth or respect God's purpose for her body, in my opinion is a predator. When he is finished with his selfish and godless acts, he disposes of the fractured female like a used paper cup.

This sounds crude, but the mentality of the sexual predator is such that he rarely views the woman as being any more valuable than a disposable item.

What happened to the time when women made a man prove his love and respect before they gave themselves to him? Whatever happened to a man making a serious commitment and informing the family of his honorable intentions? Today, guys are enjoying the pleasures of beautiful women with no commitment or act of devotion.

The original dude, Adam, gave up his rib for his woman before he ever met her! In other words, God established the system that a man must sacrifice for his woman.

Adam bled for Eve before she bled for him. Today, many brothers are seeking sex, cooking, cleaning, and the bearing of children without even an engagement. What happened?

AN EXCLUSIVE COVENANT

To a healthy, heterosexual man, the most valued thing on earth is a woman! She is way up there with oxygen and money. Actually, women are on top of the list, because a man only wants money and oxygen to be able to afford to be with a woman.

When a female gives a man sex, she has offered him the ultimate gift. This should never happen without a clear and proven demonstration of an exclusive covenant.

Speaking of the power of sex to a man, I am reminded of a situation with Lisa and me. We went to Breckenridge Ski Resort in Colorado. The high altitude got the best of me and I had to, acquire an oxygen machine to sleep with because I struggled to breathe.

Later that night, in bed, I noticed that Lisa turned her back to me and was attempting to go to sleep. I touched her in a way that she knew I had nothing but loving intentions on my mind.

Now remember, I have the oxygen machine running and the tube is in my nose. Not a pretty picture! She abruptly turned to me and asked, "What are you touching me for? Man, you can't even breathe."

I smiled and told her, "If I'm going to die, I am going out happy."

While I had all types of physical complications from the altitude, I was not going to allow it to stop me from intimacy with my wife. I would risk my health to experience her love.

If sex means that much to a man, why offer it to someone who has given nothing to you? The Bible defines and demonstrates the type of covenant a woman should enter into.

First, he must be husband material. If he cannot be or does not show interest in being such, he is a waste of your valuable time.

Scripture states, *"Husbands, love your wives, even as Christ also loved the church, and gave himself for it"* (Ephesians 5:25).

Paul is laying out a basic characteristic of a man who qualifies to be a husband. He must be willing to give of himself as Christ gave of Himself.

A woman should never be so carried away by the lure of a relationship that she fails to determine the quality of the man. Is he anxious to take you to bed, yet makes excuses about taking you to church? Will he pay for a hotel, but little else? If he's given you a baby but hesitates to give you an engagement ring, he may not be the one.

In the physical aspect of the sexual act, the woman is a receiver while the man is a giver; but, in the emotional aspect, it is reversed; the man is taking while the woman is giving.

When a woman gives herself to a man,

sexually, she is putting three major things on the line, (1) her reputation, (2) her health, and (3) her mind or emotions.

Some men can walk away from an illicit encounter and feel nothing but a perverted pride. On the other hand, when a woman has given herself to a man who has no respect or honorable intentions towards her, her self-esteem and sense of worth is negatively impacted.

The significance of a woman freely offering her body to men casually is that she is retaining a part of every man she is with in her mind, spirit, and body. There are "soul ties" developed in every sexual encounter.

God's Word says, *"What? know ye not that he which is joined to an harlot is one body? for two, saith he, shall be one flesh"* (1 Corinthians 6:16). When a man lies with a woman, he stays in her consciousness, her spirit, and he remains in her blood stream.

It's true. A man has direct access to the woman's blood stream in the sexual act—and blood always speaks of life and covenant. A virgin bleeds when she is entered for the first time. This is because a woman was never designed to give her body access to anyone other than a man to whom she was in marital covenant.

59

> *The strongest test of a man's*
> *real intentions and worthiness is his*
> *ability to wait to have sex.*

This is important for some very serious reasons. If he is unable to bridle his sexual passion, it means that he is controlled by lust.

Remember: a man who is consumed by carnal cravings will never be faithful long term. He will, at some point, become disinterested in his sexual experiences with you and look for new conquests.

Also, a man who does not have control of his sexual passions may not be able to be trusted around children.

What makes certain adults sexually abuse children? What causes some men to sexually abuse their own children? LUST is the generator of these social perversions.

It is extremely important for a woman to test a man in this area because any person you sleep with has to potentially be parent material. You do not want a man who is addicted to lust to have authority over you and your children.

This weakness is a satanic and demonic power that renders the host incapacitated. A man that cannot control his sexual passions is not a good candidate for a husband or father.

Pay attention to this scriptural warning: *"But every man is tempted, when he is drawn away of his own lust, and enticed. Then when lust hath conceived, it bringeth forth sin: and sin, when it is finished, bringeth forth death"* (James 1:14-15).

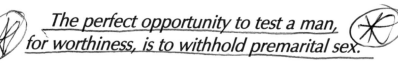

The perfect opportunity to test a man, for worthiness, is to withhold premarital sex.

If the person who has stolen your heart can be consistent and recognize the weightier matters concerning you and not stray, you then begin to get a glimpse of his character.

I believe that God, the Father, indirectly shows us this model in the man that he chose to be the earthly guardian of His son Jesus, Mary's fiancée, Joseph.

Mary was an engaged virgin. She chose a man who was committed to her without their having sex.

Here is an important question: *Why didn't God just find a virgin who didn't have a man in her life?*

I believe that Joseph was a model of what every woman should seek when choosing a partner to submit her life, body, and children to. Joseph was a secure person who was in control of his sexual passions.

He had to subdue his natural urges and had to

61

withstand public ridicule. Joseph had to support what he could not understand and love Mary unconditionally before he ever got to lie with her.

How many men do you know who will pass all of those tests before experiencing a woman sexually? Sadly, not many. This is largely due to the fact that generations of women have sold themselves too cheaply and men are conditioned to expect it for nothing. Remember, if a man cannot wait for sex, he does not qualify to be in your marital bed.

THE RIGHT MAN

My brother, pastor Samuel Blakes, has a teaching entitled, "How to Know the Right Man." He unpacks certain principles from Jesus' encounter with the woman at the well, using God's Son as the example.

It is based on this insightful account:

He [Jesus] left Judaea, and departed again into Galilee. And he must needs go through Samaria. Then cometh he to a city of Samaria, which is called Sychar, near to the parcel of ground that Jacob gave to his son Joseph. Now Jacob's well was there. Jesus therefore, being wearied with his journey, sat thus on the well: and it was about the sixth hour.

There cometh a woman of Samaria to draw water: Jesus saith unto her, Give me to drink (for his disciples were gone away unto the city to buy meat).

Then saith the woman of Samaria unto him, How is it that thou, being a Jew, askest drink of me, which am a woman of Samaria? for the Jews have no dealings with the Samaritans.

Jesus answered and said unto her, If thou knewest the gift of God, and who it is that saith to thee, Give me to drink; thou wouldest have asked of him, and he would have given thee living water.

The woman saith unto him, Sir, thou hast nothing to draw with, and the well is deep: from whence then hast thou that living water? Art thou greater than our father Jacob, which gave us the well, and drank thereof himself, and his children, and his cattle?

Jesus answered and said unto her, Whosoever drinketh of this water shall thirst again: But whosoever drinketh of the water that I shall give him shall never thirst; but the water that I shall give him shall be in him a well of water springing up into everlasting life.

The woman saith unto him, Sir, give me this water, that I thirst not, neither come hither to draw (John 4:3-15).

This story is a blueprint for what the right man with godly intentions will do in a woman's life. When you read this story in its full context, you realize this woman had been abused by men. She had drifted from one elicit relationship to another.

 THREE IMPORTANT LESSONS

The first lesson we learn from Jesus about the actions of a God-sent Man is that **He goes out of His way to meet you where you are.**

Jesus discerned that He needed to go through Samaria, which was off the traditional route of Jews because the Jews and Samaritans did not get along.

He made a detour and went out of His way to encounter this woman and to meet her needs. Remember, the Bible says, *"he must needs go through Samaria."*

The second thing Jesus teaches us is revealed in the fact that she was not there when he first arrived. But Jesus sat down and waited for her.

The right man will wait on you.

The third thing we see Jesus doing is that He understood her past and accepted her just the same.

 The right man will accept you unconditionally for who you are.

Finally, we see Jesus exchanging spiritual water for natural water with her. The woman had been focused on surface issues while Jesus addressed something that was lacking deep in her soul. He satisfied a thirst that had never before truly been quenched.

 The right man will satisfy your heart.

He will touch your soul and mind before he reaches for your body.

This woman of the world was made whole by encountering a Man who loved her with the love of God. She had been broken over and over again by men who used her body for lustful means.

If a man cannot heal your hurts, erase your failures, accept you as you are, and be patient enough to wait on you, he does not deserve you. The right person must have the potential to love your mind and spirit without any consideration for your body. He has to possess the capacity to love you as Christ loved the church.

The Lord gave Himself for the church long before the church reciprocated.

The right man will present himself and wait patiently for you to respond. He never pressures, threatens, or demands ultimatums. The right man lovingly gives of himself to the point that it is a natural response for you to submit your mind and body to him as priest of your life.

This is why I say, both spiritually and physically, never lay your body down for a man who has not laid down his life for you.

CHAPTER 4

NEVER BE WITH A MAN WHO MAKES YOU AFRAID

No woman was created to be abused at the hands of a sick man.

The reality of abuse is more prevalent than the church wants to accept. A man who will behave aggressively towards a woman does not deserve her presence. In fact, a real man will never put his hands on a woman in anger. Little boys fight with girls, but grown men don't fight with women. An abusive man is simply an angry little boy.

The Bible counsels: *"Likewise, ye husbands, dwell with them according to knowledge, giving honour unto the wife, as unto the weaker vessel, and as being heirs together of the grace of life; that your prayers be not hindered"* (1 Peter 3:7).

The definition of *honor* in the original Greek is *tee-may*—which means to value, esteem to the highest degree, or handle as precious.

It is advisable that every woman pay very close attention to the level of frustration a man portrays when things are not going well. A woman should

also take very seriously a man's short temper. If he does not honor you in the small things, he has the potential to ultimately dishonor you in the worst possible way.

As a woman, there are certain things that you simply cannot tolerate. Abuse and terror are high on the list. No woman needs a man so badly that she lives in constant fear just to have him around.

The Absence of Anxiety

My father, Bishop Robert Blakes, Sr., always taught my brother and me that we were never to be forceful towards women. As a child, I don't remember one incident where my father introduced fear into our home. I was never afraid for daddy to come home.

I have never been awakened by the sound of my father beating my mother. I don't know what it is to witness my father verbally assault my mother.

The most interesting fact is that he never raised his hands, never used abrasive language, or rarely raised his voice, and my mother honored him as head of the house.

Every woman must know that a man who is controlling and obnoxious is too insecure to be head of anything. God did not create the woman to be handled by the man physically or dominated emotionally. As the Bible states, *"Husbands, love your wives, and be not bitter against them"* (Colossians 3:19). Scripture disapproves of abusive men.

The unfortunate truth is that society has begun to glamorize the abuse of women by men. The current glorification of "pimping," in the inner cities of America only serves to precondition a new generation of young boys to become abusive men that control their women by any means necessary.

The real question is: *why do women allow themselves to be put in the position to be mistreated and terrorized by the men they sleep with?*

Why accept so little from someone to whom you're giving everything? I believe that this is becoming more prevalent because we have fewer women who are raised with a father who is in place spiritually, emotionally, and financially.

Generally, a woman who has a strong fatherly support system has greater courage and intolerance for the violence of any man.

When a woman has not had the support of a father in her life, she is empty in certain places and is rendered vulnerable. She is conditioned to feel that she has no choice but to accept what the stronger male society heaps upon her.

SOME WOMEN ALLOW FINANCIAL SECURITY TO TRAP THEM IN AN ABUSIVE RELATIONSHIP

As a pastor, I have discovered that many women are imprisoned to toxic relationships because they are financially dependent. A woman is always running the risk of being totally reliant on a man. The ideal of the man being the bread winner and truly taking care of his wife lovingly and honorably is for the most part over. Today a woman has to have a plan B.

For women who are in abusive situations where they have been trapped by the economic arrangement, I say, "God is your provider."

Never settle for less, trying to hold onto a few

70

dollars. You must ask yourself the question, "Is this really worth it?"

This trap takes a toll on your self-esteem. Plus, the damage that is done to your health and the psychological imprint the abuse is making on your children are too high of a cost to settle. God can take care of you!

Boldly say with the writer of Hebrews: *"The Lord is my helper, and I will not fear what man shall do unto me"* (Hebrews 13:6).

The first step out of an abusive relationship is facing the fear. In the movie, "What's Love Got to Do With It?" once Tina stood her ground and fought Ike back, he never attempted to hit her again.

When you awaken to the fact that you are no longer afraid of this man, you will soon discover he's been a coward the entire time.

Likewise, if you saw the movie, "The Color Purple," once Miss Celie mustered up enough boldness to confront "Mr." (or Albert as he is occasionally called), she uncovered the gutless wimp he had been all along.

One person put it this way, "Far better to die on your feet than to live on your knees."

A MAN WHO HURTS YOU DOES NOT LOVE YOU

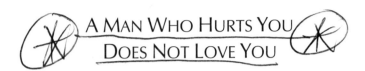

A woman can become so conditioned to abuse that she may begin to define it as real love. Some have been so immersed into dysfunctional relationships that they actually view aggressive male behavior as a demonstration of affection.

Right now, commit this verse to memory: *"There is no fear in love; but perfect love casteth out fear: because fear hath torment. He that feareth is not made perfect in love"* (1 John 4:18).

When a man truly loves a woman, he may become angry, but will never frighten her. Any person who makes you afraid is not sent from God and does not deserve the honor of your presence.

You wouldn't put your life at risk and drive a car that you were afraid would explode. You wouldn't own and bring into your home a large dog that you knew to be vicious. So why keep a man who acts like a ticking time bomb?

Another factor that keeps women stuck in bad relationships is that men often blame their behavior on their own personal struggles. For instance, a man may try justifying his actions by saying, "I hit you because I'm stressed out on my job." Or, "I have a drug problem."

There is nowhere in the Bible or in the realm of common sense where a woman is to put herself in jeopardy because of another person's issues. You should leave him to work on his problems and not remain in the line of fire in the name of love.

I remember as a child that my father struggled with alcoholism. Thankfully, because of an encounter with the Holy Spirit, he was supernaturally set free from his addiction. He went on be become a world renowned leader and advocate for sobriety and God's power to heal. But when he was a practicing alcoholic, he drank every day.

He would wreck cars and stay out all night. My brother and I would have to drag him from the vehicle and put him in his bed. Yet, during all those times, he never placed his hand on our mother. He never cursed at her and was never physically abusive towards us. My point is that alcohol did not alter his base character.

If a man beats you when he's drunk, that is simply who he is at the core.

Finally, women get caught on the "wish upon a star" trip. You want to stay because you just believe that something is going to change soon. Well, in many cases, it's been over ten years;

73

when is soon coming.

A woman has to become intolerant of promises, wishes, and hopes. At some point, you have to call it what it is and bury a dead situation. Even Jesus put time limits on certain matters. Consider the parable of the fig tree:

> *A certain man had a fig tree planted in his vineyard; and he came and sought fruit thereon, and found none. Then said he unto the dresser of his vineyard, Behold, these three years I come seeking fruit on this fig tree, and find none: cut it down; why cumbereth it the ground?*
>
> *And he answering said unto him, Lord, let it alone this year also, till I shall dig about it, and dung it: and if it bear fruit, well: and if not, then after that thou shalt cut it down* (Luke 13:6-9)

When something is occupying space and consuming resources, it should yield fruit. This is especially true in terms of relationships. How can you give your all yet see no progress? You are still going through the same things you began with. How much time are you willing to give before you cut it down?

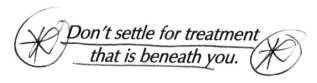

Don't settle for treatment that is beneath you.

Consider this testimony of an anonymous Caucasian woman:

> I entered into a relationship with a man who appeared to be the finest of gentlemen. He did all of the right things, from opening doors to buying flowers and remembering special days.
>
> A strange twist came when he was terminated from his job and did not have the financial means to continue his accustomed lifestyle. I then learned that he associated his self-identity with his occupation and his self-worth to the size of his paycheck. He began to resent me for providing for the family.
>
> He initially became withdrawn and it went on to snapping and complaining about everything. It ultimately morphed into physical assaults accompanied with verbal bashings. He would call me every vulgar name imaginable as he kicked and hit me.
>
> He would always cry and apologize after every episode. I actually stayed in this cycle for five years.

The eye-opening moment for me was the day I walked in on my oldest daughter, eight years old at the time, attempting to teach her younger brother how a man was to beat a woman. Unfortunately, my children were being conditioned by my experiences to become victims and victimizers. In essence I abused my kids by living as a victim.

I called the authorities that day and have never looked back.

Sadly, the story of this woman is being repeated in millions of lives across our world at this very moment.

 Now is the time to stand up and put a stop to abuse. With God's help your life can change for the better.

CHAPTER 5

A WOMAN MUST ALWAYS BE PREPARED TO EARN HER OWN MONEY

When reading the Bible, we often search for deep meanings and profound sayings. But, for the most part, God's Word is a book filled with principles of common sense.

One such principle states, *"...the borrower is servant to the lender"* (Proverbs 22:7).

When we look at this truth, in relation to women today, it is not hard to draw the conclusion that every woman should strive to be employable and self-sufficient when possible.

This is the wrong era for a woman to be in a position of depending on others for her life's sustainability.

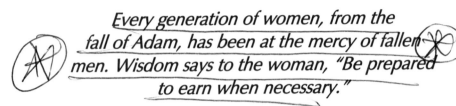

Every generation of women, from the fall of Adam, has been at the mercy of fallen men. Wisdom says to the woman, "Be prepared to earn when necessary."

It is an ongoing tragedy because, to a large extent, women are still hoping for an ideal that died long ago. Yet many cling to the concept that a man will provide financially and simply take care of the wife.

However, the stark reality is that the current generation of men are not raised or conditioned to even *desire* the role of sole provider.

When a wife throws all of her financial hopes onto the weak shoulders of an inept and unwilling man, she tragically sets herself up for major disappointment and hardship.

Today, a woman must make education and personal ambition a priority. For her to have the ability to provide for herself is a matter of self-preservation, especially in a time when divorce is as common as marriage and unfaithful men are the majority. It makes sense that every woman be able to secure her future by making herself financially viable on her own terms.

Because females have traditionally taken a financially passive role in their relationships with men, many have even failed to exercise fiscal responsibility as single women. They make the excuse, "Don't worry. I'll find a man who will take care of me." They are looking for "Mr. Right" who will provide and pamper them.

This mindset reveals itself in those who spend untold sums of hard-earned money on clothes, cosmetology, and entertainment. Some do this with no concern for saving or investing into an uncertain tomorrow. But the day soon dawns when she is living in a constant state of lack and stress.

Why do many women behave so irresponsibly? In their socially conditioned minds, they believe that eventually a man will come riding in on a white horse, sweep them off their feet and meet all of their needs. This false assumption positions them emotionally to live footloose and fancy free today; because tomorrow their prince will arrive. How sad when he never shows up!

 CLOSING THE FINANCIAL GAP

The Washington Post Family Foundation recently polled 2,000 individuals and found that nearly three quarters of black women worry they won't have enough money to pay their bills. The study also showed a disproportionate gap between black women and white women.

Research reveals that while single white women ages 36-49 have a median wealth or total asset value of $42,600, single black women have a median net wealth of about $5. That's total assets—cash in the bank, stocks, bonds and real estate, minus debts.

Of course, there are many institutional factors that explain why African American women are so impoverished; but on that list is the fact that many women are conditioned to be financially reckless.

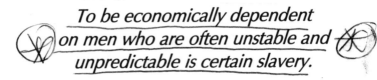

To be economically dependent on men who are often unstable and unpredictable is certain slavery.

The passage at the beginning of this chapter about the borrower being a slave to the lender makes it clear that the one with the money is the boss. As the old saying goes, "The golden rule is: he that has the gold makes the rules."

Of course, we are not encouraging cynical thinking in the minds of women, but we are promoting caution and preparation. Should a woman be fortunate enough to have a respectful provider for a husband, that's wonderful. But even under ideal circumstances, one cannot find any sensible argument against every woman striving to position herself to be self-sustaining, if necessary.

It is better to have the capability and not need it than to need it and not have it.

The power of a woman to be able to earn is far more important than personal security; it can be a matter of dominion.

Many want a king for a man while maintaining a peasant's mentality. The reality is, most kings are looking for a queen.

A queen has the capacity to hold her own. She only multiplies the total impact when they are together. In Proverbs, the story of the virtuous woman and her husband models the king and queen dynamic. *"Her husband is known in the gates, when he sitteth among the elders of the land. She maketh fine linen, and selleth it; and delivereth girdles unto the merchant"* (Proverbs 31:23-24).

This woman's husband was a well-connected person of power and means. In spite of his acclaim, she still found a way to make some money on her own accord.

NICKELS AND DIMES

Our most recent examples of First Ladies of the United States set a powerful and polarizing precedent. Whereas previous generations of presidential wives have been the "stand by your man" types, Hillary Clinton and Michelle Obama have established a unique standard for modern women. In both cases, they are as brilliant as, and possibly more dynamic, than their husbands. Also, their spouses testify that they would not have achieved all they had without their resourceful wives.

Great men are no longer looking for the helpless damsel; they are searching for the powerful partner.

Lyfe Jennings penned some very powerful lyrics to young women in one of his songs when he wrote, "Don't be a nickel looking for a dime."

He was teaching young females to establish and know their worth and to not settle for less.

A young lady should increase her personal worth if she wants a certain type of guy. Nickels rarely have the capacity to attract dimes.

> *The most significant thing a single woman can do is to improve herself spiritually, physically and financially.*

It is true that: "We do not attract what we want or deserve; we attract what we are."

In Old Testament days, Esther saw herself as a

queen, and as a consequence, she caught the attention of a king. She had the position before she had the title. To appeal to the best man, be the best woman possible.

I pride myself on being able to provide for my wife; but one of my greatest joys is to say that my wife can easily provide for herself without me. This is a blessing because life is too uncertain.

A man's capacity to provide may be impacted at any moment. What is a woman and her family to do in the interim?

IN THE MIDST OF THE STORM

I vividly remember when Hurricane Katrina devastated the city of New Orleans and our ministry there. We evacuated and eventually landed in Houston, Texas. I did not know what the future of our ministry would be in the city of New Orleans. I had no clue if I would ever be able to provide for my wife again as she had been accustomed.

I will never forget her words to me. She said, "I can get a job to sustain us."

Wow! What if I had married just a pretty face? It was extremely gratifying to know that my wife could provide—and *would* if necessary.

A man who truly loves his spouse would desire

for her to be independent of him financially. It should never be viewed as an affront to his manhood if she is capable of carrying the financial load. In fact, any husband who feels it necessary for his woman to diminish for him to excel is far less than a worthy man.

It is alarming how many times I encounter women who refuse to buy homes or apply for promotions because they are fearful that their success will dissuade a potential male suitor. Any man who requires a woman to be deficient is unworthy of occupying a position of headship in her life.

As for me and my three girls, I have always encouraged financial independence. I never want my daughters to be at the mercy of any man.

A POSITIVE EXAMPLE

Let me share the story of a mother of two independent young women:

I have two girls, Nicole and Monique. They are blessed to have a strong father in their lives. Not a casual or occasional father, but an ever-present figure, supporting our family in every way.

Financially, they never went without, but

in addition, his presence provided structure, discipline and the security of knowing they were valued and loved. They saw themselves through his eyes, and his support instilled confidence in everything they did because they knew he had their back.

The girls did not need to seek their worth through the attention of young men. They knew they were his beautiful princesses because he told them so, often. He was a man of faith and led by example, bringing the entire family to church most Sundays. This helped them to develop a deep-seeded faith, and setting God as a priority that still guides their lives today.

My girls were not overly influenced by their friends, adhering most times to our core values. And when they faced a challenge, they often sought guidance from their father first. As a father, he reinforced my efforts. And through him they saw an example of a father working within the family unit.

He supported them academically and stressed the importance of education and hard work. He showed them, by example, how a man should treat and respect a woman and not cause physical harm, even in times of disagreement.

Today, my girls are grown, 22 and 25, and have evolved into very strong, intelligent and beautiful young women. One has received her Masters degree in public health and works for a major energy company. The other will soon graduate with her Bachelor's degree in engineering and plans to go to medical school. Neither has married and both have decided to wait to marry until they finish their education and establish their careers.

Neither has a child out of wedlock; neither has been in trouble with the law; and both have a deep respect for authority and a reverence for God. For that, I am grateful, and we are all truly blessed.

I am sure their father's presence has made all the difference. Today, they still maintain a good relationship with their dad, speaking with him often and keeping him abreast of the happenings in their adult life. They share their achievements and discuss their challenges, knowing that he will have a warm embrace for them in either case.

I am sure that he will continue to have an impact on their decisions, the men that they choose to marry, and the way that they see themselves in the world.

– A loving mother, Marcia Bent Henry,
PhD, Biochemistry

VIRTUE OR VICTIM?

The importance of a woman who maximizes her personal financial capacity is a serious matter. The Bible highlights the benefits of the virtuous woman of Proverbs 31 and her approach to life. She had a prolific husband and yet she expanded her own personal economic opportunities. Her mate could carry the family's needs and yet she valued keeping herself sharp and current in terms of her personal earning power. A woman must never be in a position of helplessness financially.

Society is not kind to helpless women.

The contrast to the virtuous woman of Proverbs 31 is the widow woman of 2 Kings 4. Her husband was a man of God, but he died prematurely and left his family in debt. As a consequence, the creditors were preparing to take his sons as slaves to repay the money owed. His wife and family were now in crisis mode because of his failure of a financial plan. The wife, who apparently relied totally on him for financial stability, was now exposed. Circumstances had forced her out of her daydream. She now had to face real life financial matters for herself.

As Scripture records:

Now there cried a certain woman of the wives of the sons of the prophets unto Elisha, saying, Thy servant my husband is dead; and thou knowest that thy servant did fear the Lord: and the creditor is come to take unto him my two sons to be bondmen.

Elisha said unto her, What shall I do for thee? tell me, what hast thou in the house? And she said, Thine handmaid hath not any thing in the house, save a pot of oil.

Then he said, Go, borrow thee vessels abroad of all thy neighbors, even empty vessels; borrow not a few. And when thou art come in, thou shalt shut the door upon thee and upon thy sons, and shalt pour out into all those vessels, and thou shalt set aside that which is full.

So she went from him, and shut the door upon her and upon her sons, who brought the vessels to her; and she poured out. And it came to pass, when the vessels were full, that she said unto her son, Bring me yet a vessel.

And he said unto her, There is not a vessel more. And the oil stayed. Then she came and told the man of God. And he said, Go, sell the oil, and pay thy debt, and live thou and thy children of the rest (2 Kings 4:1-7).

What stands out to me in this text is that it took a crisis for this widow to get out of her chair and to seek to maximize financially. She had wasted years hiding out in the background of her husband's possible ineptness.

What if she had sought a debt elimination strategy while he lived? What if she had financial counsel before he died? The story may have ended quite differently.

I am fully aware that there are many men who are intimidated by a woman who seeks to pursue financial independence. If you are dating an antiquated caveman like this, dump him and move on. He obviously doesn't have your best interest at heart.

A real man always wants his woman to be able to survive in the event something happens to him personally or to his earning power.

A man who would keep a woman dependent on his coin purse is a controller.

Don't let the months and years pass you by. Create a plan for financial independence and keep working toward this goal.

Remember, it is better to have the capability and not need it than to need it and not have it.

CHAPTER 6

MOST MEN WILL SAY ANYTHING FOR SEX

One of the great mysteries of the times is that young women remain ignorant regarding the devices of malicious young men, even though the game has been the same for thousands of years.

Why don't women know better? Why can't they simply recognize the tendencies? Why do the same woman fall for the same tricks repeatedly with different men? Why?

Perhaps this verse applies: *"My people are destroyed for lack of knowledge: because thou hast rejected knowledge, I will also reject thee"* (Hosea 4:6).

Women generally fall prey to the misdealings of men for this exact reason: they either lack or reject the truth.

Far too often a woman clearly sees that a man

91

has no noble intentions, yet she ignores the elephant in the room, simply hoping she can convince him to be the one.

Much of this knowledge relative to men is designed to come from the instruction of a father who, ideally, should have been in place. That father may be biological, surrogate, or spiritual. The problem is that a woman is rarely compliant with the instruction of a father about a man she is interested in. She won't listen! Because a dad is typically resistant to the idea of his daughter entertaining *any* man, she adopts a policy of exclusion pertaining to her father and her relational choices.

When a woman believes she is in love, there's almost nothing that can get through to her to change her mind. She enters into a zombie-like zone and trance, hears no logic, does not receive any instruction, and believes everything that a man tells her. She is in a position of willful ignorance.

The Bible warns, *"There is a way which seemeth right unto a man, the end thereof are the ways of death"* (Proverbs 14:22).

The lovelorn woman bases her actions on emotions, not realizing that an experienced man knows how to make her feel just as he wants her to. Many men are like magicians; they manipulate the perception of people to see what they want seen.

As Paul wrote to young Timothy, *"For of this sort are they which creep into houses, and lead captive silly women laden with sins, led away with divers lusts"* (2 Timothy 3:6).

The term, *silly*, in the Greek means "a foolish woman; one who displays immaturity and a lack of dignity."

This text highlights two facts pertaining to a silly woman. First, she is sought out by deceptive men. Second, she is easily led astray. I pray this does not describe your situation.

When will women grow up and stop being so credulous? It seems to be the way of humanity. Those who will avoid many problems are the ones who honor and respect the role of fathers in their lives. As they hear and heed his words, they will become mature beyond the deceits of pointless men.

We reach maturity in one of two ways: by instruction or experience.

When a woman is not exposed to fatherly instruction early, it leads her to a lifetime of experiences which can leave her broken, used, and bitter.

Often, the difference between a wise, healthy, discerning woman versus a silly, gullible girl that is used as a sex toy, is the father's advice about men and sexuality.

A responsible father should make it clear to his daughters that a man will say anything to get his way sexually.

It's no secret that women are moved by touching and poignant words. Men have figured this phenomenon out and have mastered the technique of wooing.

Wooing is the art of using a lot of flowery words to actually say nothing; but it is designed to make a woman believe everything.

A man will say whatever it takes to disarm a woman emotionally and spiritually to compromise her sexually.

There is an intense lust in an immature man to which women usually cannot relate. He will say anything to have his way with the woman's body. He will promise, "I love you; I will marry you." Even, "God told me that you are the one."

He is driven by lust.

About this sin, Jesus stated, *"Whosoever looketh on a woman to lust after her hath committed adultery with her already in his heart"* (Matthew 5:28).

It's interesting that the text specifies men as the lusters. This is because men are carried away with this powerful force that generates an insatiable desire. This passion produces predictable behaviors such as lying, deception, and manipulation.

A woman is different. She has to move from acquaintance, to friendship, to attraction, and then to sex. A man, however, usually is driven straight to sex. He doesn't need to know her family, likes, dislikes, where she is from or what her goals in life might be. He just wants to sleep with her.

> **_The crisis for women is that the man's salacious motivation can disguise itself as friendship and commitment until he gets what he wants._**

Even young boys are raised to deceive females. We learn in the barber shop, at family reunions, or anywhere we find older men, what to say and how to behave deceptively to attain the desired outcome, which is sex.

We are taught to lie about how much money we make because financial security is very important to a woman. We are trained to act patient and thoughtful because the opposite sex loves a man who is sensitive. We even learn to go to church and behave like we really love God. Many women want a spiritual partner who holds to biblical ethics and values. However, in many

95

cases, it amounts to nothing more than an act. We learned the script when we were young.

When the man accomplishes his intent, his character changes like the Hulk. He morphs into a monster of some kind. Once the sexual act is complete, the male who was so thoughtful, spiritual, and sensitive won't even want to hold the same woman in the same bed in which he just copulated with her.

This becomes a very sad awakening for the gullible young woman. It is when she has given herself to a man who played a role that she discovers he was only acting.

After he has taken everything from her, she has to face the fact that, in his eyes, she was no more than prey. He said all the right things, but will back up none of them. He has used her and he is now finished! Tragic!

"IF I HAD LISTENED"

Allow me to share the words of a woman who will remain nameless:

I have had twenty-five sexual partners in a life that is just over four decades long. It started out when I was a teenager.
I believed that I could make a man love

me if I gave him what he wanted. I did everything that was asked of me for many men and none of them ever stayed. I had high hopes, from one relationship to the next, that this would be the one. It never happened.

I was always so convinced that their words were true. For some reason, my judgment was non-existent.

Today, I have physical female complications because of so much sexual activity. I have no children and I struggle with relationships. It is so hard for me to believe anything a man says because I've been lied to so many times.

The few honest men who have tried to enter my life have been turned off by my anger and emotional baggage. If I had listened to my mother I would have preserved myself for the man who would have been willing to wait for me.

Women, wake up! Recognize lies and deceit for what they are. Set your standards high and never allow them to be lowered.

God can erase your past and allow you to start over again. Yes, you can become the worthy prize of an honorable, godly man.

CHAPTER 7

ONCE A MAN HAS A WOMAN'S BODY, HE IS IN HER SOUL

When a woman gives herself sexually to a man, she is tied to that individual for life. It's called a soul tie.

DEFINITION: A soul tie is an emotional bondage to another person that prohibits the individual (in this case the woman) from moving on.

When a male engages a female sexually, he occupies a part of her soul. The word *soul* in the Greek New Testament is *psuche*. Its meaning is the heart, will, and emotions of the person.

The woman who surrenders herself sexually to an illicit man (one other than her husband) is sacrificing her emotional well-being and health.

As we read statistics, watch intrusive television shows, and listen to the cries of women in society, we can only conclude that those who are emotionally damaged are in their situation because of some illicit sexual connection with an ungodly man. They are either broken because they were violated against their will, or they have been victimized by men they chose, who misrepresented themselves.

As a consequence, the woman becomes hardened and often begins to behave in a manner that leads her life down a path of perpetual problems.

Ungodly men will discern a woman's fractured soul and worm their way into her life, pretending to be the one who will be her savior, rescuing her from the pain of the past. Against better judgment, the woman is opened to a sexual relationship, even with this man, because she is hopeful that he, finally, is the exception to the rule and will heal her wounds and mend her broken heart.

However, at the end of the affair she finds herself disappointed once more. The sad reality is that this scene is repeated over and over again.

Many young women who are drawn into prostitution are initially captured because the pimp (one who sells another for sex) nurtures what feels like a supportive relationship. He seems to sympathize, promises to provide financially, and offers to protect her. This leads to her falling in love and giving herself to him sexually.

Once he has sufficiently invaded her psyche through sex, he begins to control and manipulate her emotionally and physically. He also seduces her into a position of financial dependency. So often, she is carried away with his lies and charm and will do anything for him—including selling her body.

This same godless principle applies to everyday relationships. While the men may not be pimps, they acquire control of a woman's will and psyche through the intimacy of perverted sex.

When a woman gives her body, she is giving her all.

There is a distinct difference between how men and women process failed sexual relationships. When a strong personal bond is broken, the man often counts it as another notch on his belt, while the woman is scarred for life. She is left trying to reconstruct her self-worth while he gains bragging rights about his conquest.

This part is difficult for me to write, and I am not proud of my previous actions, but I think it will help to open the eyes of some young women. I've already confessed to my scandalous past and womanizing.

The following occurred decades after I had turned that unfortunate history of my early life around. I was now older, wiser, and spiritually committed to my marriage and ministry.

I was sitting in a public place when a middle-aged woman approached, acting as if she knew me. That was not unusual because I am often recognized from television, those who have visited our church or conferences, etc.

The conversation became a bit uncomfortable when she suggested that I should remember details about who she was and other aspects of her life. Honestly, I didn't have a clue who I was talking to.

Finally the brief chance meeting ended and she walked away, visibly hurt. I replayed that unusual conversation over and over in my mind all evening, and then it hit me like a bolt of lightning!

I recalled vague memories of this lady from more than two decades earlier. She was a person whom I had intimate relations with when I was much younger. I had come face to face with a person from my past, yet I didn't immediately remember her—even though she clearly knew me.

It was now a generation later and I was

obviously still living in her mind while I had moved on with my life. I was no longer the person she remembered.

To face the fact that this woman was living with a negative memory that stemmed from my youthful failures was heartbreaking. When a woman thinks that the transaction in a sexual experience, outside of marriage, is equal between her and a man she is self-deceived.

Another way a woman's mind is impacted, after a casual sexual encounter, is that society views both parties very differently. After the brief affair, as unjust as it may seem, he's a barber shop hero while the woman is labeled a community whore. She has to process this stigma and newfound reputation as she moves about in circles that know the details of the relationship. What she thought was the real thing turned out to be nothing but a fling.

When relationships end, men move on while women are often ostracized in society.

There is a biblical example of the stigma and social outcast that women experience when they have been manipulated sexually.

While Jesus walked on earth, *"the scribes and Pharisees brought unto him a woman taken in adultery; and when they had set her in the midst, they said unto him, Master, this woman was taken in the very act"* (John 8:3-4).

Every time I read this text, the same question springs to mind: Where was the man?"

If they caught her in the act of adultery, it means that there was a man on the scene as well. Where was he?

Society usually frowns on a woman who has given herself to a person outside of covenant, yet celebrates a man who has overcome a woman's sense of better judgment, self-respect, and common sense to steal her most precious resource, herself. She then has to live with the fact that she's given her all to one who has returned nothing but pain and shame.

> **When a man has a woman outside of covenant, he tampers with her self-respect, reputation, and sense of honor.**

The psychological fallout of illicit sex leaves even the strongest of women with compromised self-esteem.

The most heartbreaking reality of a person who has been victimized by a non-ordained relationship is that it can impair her ability to recognize the right man when he enters her life.

When Mr. Right shows up, she often drives him away because her lenses are so clouded with the filth of the past. Sad but true, when a woman has known nothing but the wrong men, she loses her capacity to appreciate the one who is right.

Your heart and soul are precious to God, make certain they are also precious to you.

CHAPTER 8

A REAL MAN WILL ALWAYS SETTLE WITH A WOMAN HE RESPECTS

There's something very consistent in the nature of men, and many women miss it. It is the fact that they will play around for years with loose and easy women, then will suddenly marry a person who respected herself enough to demand he respect her.

 A woman who does not yield easily will reserve a place of honor in his heart.

When a young lady does not understand this reality, she may have a tendency to loosen her moral stance and acquiesce to what she assumes to be the man's desire. She will cave in sexually because she believes this is the way to win him over. This is a tragic mistake.

There are many popular reality shows that depict women as overtly sexual, easy, drunken, violent, and available to the highest bidder. These only serve to mislead a young woman in her management of male relationships. Pop culture sends the message loud and clear: "You must behave as a whore to compete."

 A man will pressure a woman sexually, then express disappointment when she gives in.

In this day and age, the moral scale has so plummeted that women are literally bending over backwards to win a man's acceptance. This is a slippery slope because a man will toy with a woman who has no boundaries. But when he matures, he will become serious about a girl who offered limited access. Ladies, the only attraction for a man to a woman who is free with her body is the sexual enticement. There is nothing in this scenario that signals, "Wife for life, or mother of children." It's just about the sex.

While the woman may think that the fastest way to the altar is through the bedroom, the reverse is true: the farther you climb into the bed, the farther away from the altar you move.

In this book we have spoken of the virtuous woman—a role model to which every young lady should aspire. She possesses uncommon qualities and is the one a man wants to bring home to mom; the girl he will turn his "player's" card in for. She's the person he wants to bear and influence his children and grow old with.

Her price is *"far above rubies. The heart of her husband doth safely trust in her, so that he shall have no need of spoil"* (Proverbs 31:10-11).

The husband of this virtuous woman had no questions about his wife's integrity, loyalty, or honesty. She exhibited such a self-respecting lifestyle that she gave her spouse no choice but to see her as a woman of high value and honor.

Men are searching for a virtuous woman, yet she is becoming harder and harder to find.

Times have changed drastically since I was a younger man. The dynamics between men and women are now quite different. When I was a teen trying to learn how to manage the requirements of young ladies, it necessitated much thought and effort to even attain a minimal response of approval. I had to open doors, talk respectfully, pay for lunch, and try to act like a gentleman for a reasonable amount of time.

In today's generation, a man does not have to display much respect for women. He can expect her to "pay as she goes"—and she will willingly do so. He can demand sex before he even knows her full name, and, in many instances, she will be happy to comply.

Here's the saddest part: in far too many cases, if he behaves as a respectful gentleman, she won't be attracted to him.

The contemporary woman does not realize that the only kind of male a fast and easy woman attracts is a "dog of a man." She continues to be heartbroken time and time again and seems to never learn the lesson through the pain. The man is hoping to find a companion he can respect because she respects herself.

> **_For a woman to be considered as a wife, she must behave like one first._**

Sister, establish your standards, promote your values, and never compromise your integrity. Respect yourself because you are made in God's image.

Here are four things a woman must never do:

1. Never initiate a relationship with a man.
2. Never accept a man's word that you don't know. Ask questions.
3. Never tolerate any disrespect.
4. Never stop enforcing your boundaries.

It may be uncomfortable being the one who always says "No" and imposes limits, but it is what virtuous women do.

This is especially important if you are a Christian who lives to please God. A man may express displeasure in your convictions, but don't be swayed. A real man will ultimately admire you for your righteous resolve.

Every woman must know that looks and "curves" will fade away. Your character is for life.

As God's Word so eloquently states, *"Favor is deceitful, and beauty is vain: but a woman that feareth the Lord, she shall be praised. Give her of the fruit of her hands; and let her own works praise her in the gates"* (Proverbs 31:30-31).

I would advise every woman to resist falling head over heels for the man who does not meet you on your terms. Never be so anxious for a wedding that you perform as a wife before you have the covenant in place.

Have it etched in your mind that there are certain levels beneath which you will not stoop. You should be so resolute concerning this that you are willing to live single for the rest of your days before you allow yourself to be degraded and disrespected.

When a woman has this kind of backbone and character, she will attract God's best for her life.

Be strong and defy the urge to be carried away with emotions and feelings. Romance is a tricky sentiment, especially for a woman.

An experienced male suitor knows exactly what a woman longs to hear and will say those "trigger" words to make her drop her guard. He can make her feel like it's perfect when in fact, it is tragic. Before you know it she is swept off her feet with no consideration for her values.

A wise woman will work hard to keep her emotions in check. She will keep a level head and maintain her own self-respect. It is so easy, for even a Christian woman to be caught off guard in the heat of irrational passion.

Always remember what Scripture teaches: *"But every man is tempted, when he is drawn away of his own lust, and enticed. Then when lust hath conceived, it bringeth forth sin: and sin, when it is finished, bringeth forth death"* (James 1:14-15).

The danger in being carried away is that you may end up in an unfamiliar place.

As a lady, you never want to do anything to misrepresent yourself to your future husband. It does not take much for him to draw false conclusions about your character and to categorize you inappropriately.

It is a rare occasion that a man will be spiritually focused and mature enough to establish godly boundaries for a relationship. It is the woman's responsibility to protect her own virtue and reputation. When she does, she allows the person she is seeing to view her for who she really is.

To the extent a woman respects herself, the man is able to truly focus on her qualities as opposed to the distraction of her sexual appeal.

These are important matters to pray over in the decision-making process.

PART II

LET ME INTRODUCE YOU TO GAME 101

CHAPTER 9

THE GAMES THAT MEN PLAY

As a young man in the inner city of New Orleans, Louisiana, I grew up across the street from a very popular pimp. This was in an area called "Holly Grove."

Not only did I live near him, I had favor with this ghetto business man. We would often talk and he allowed me to explore his lifestyle of fast cars, big money, and beautiful women up close and personal. As a young urban male, before my spiritual commitment, I was captivated.

I saw how a man can entice a woman psychologically and emotionally, and from that point convince her to go in any direction of his choosing. I learned—from observing the best of the worst—what the game is and how it is played.

Many women become involved with men like this and don't fully recognize what is happening to them.

Consider this scenario:

The scene could be duplicated outside of almost any church or club in America.

There's a woman crying and a man trying to keep a straight face but can't hide the smirk. They've been dating for six months. She actually thought he was the one. She believed it so much that she cooked, cleaned, checked in, and even met his sexual needs—against her opposing Christian values and home training.

The conversation goes like this:

HIM: "I just think we need some space. Baby, I'm dealing with stuff that you wouldn't understand. It's a man thing".

HER: "What didn't I do? Where did I go wrong? How can I improve?"

HIM: "Nothing wrong with you. I'm just stressed about some things, and I need to get my head together. I'm sorry."

She's heartbroken and depressed for months and perhaps years, while he leaves that conversation to go on a date with another woman the same night.

What was the breakdown?"

She sought to make a life with him. He only sought to spend a few nights in her bed. It was merely a game!

To reiterate, a young woman should be wise and not believe everything a man says he is or appears to be. Many times, it is purely make-believe. An insightful, mature, and godly woman learns to pray about the individual she is considering and asks God to guide her with the compass of wisdom and discernment.

It's amazing what the Lord will reveal if you ask for His guidance. As Scripture tells us, *"Beloved, believe not every spirit, but try the spirits whether they are of God: because many false prophets are gone out into the world"* (1 John 4:1).

It is important for the woman to be alert and aware; because, much time may be wasted with a man who is just playing games. It's best to know the game, recognize it for what it is, and bring a swift end to playful situations.

To a great extent, we have society to blame for the dynamics of the drama men inflict on women. Our culture breeds deception into the male-female connection. We are conditioned to per-form the roles we play as men and women.

In the average American home, ideally, daugh-ters are raised to believe that a woman should maintain virginity, get married, be faithful, and have children by her husband—and that a husband and family is the ultimate accomplishment.

On the other hand, there are sons who are raised to think that being a man involves making money and managing multiple sexual relationships—often with many women at the same time. Men learn to make a game of anything, and win at whatever they do.

Many raise their sons, either directly or indirectly, to think that womanizing is natural and anything different is strange.

In our world, the man is brought up to view all of life as a competition in which he is either winning or losing, based on money, women, and toys.

The woman is taught to be chaste and faithful while the man is viewed as socially awkward if he adheres to the Christian ethic of abstinence. She is taught to refrain from sex while his peers teach him to become sexually active as soon as possible.

It doesn't make sense, but the same uncle who talks to his niece about virginity will turn around and give his nephew condoms and a graphic lesson in sex education.

The tension between male and female is created by our upbringing. She is trained to build a strong defense, while he is encouraged to break down the barriers.

The two conflicting agendas creates the necessity for deception because he (the man) has to make her (the woman) believe that he wants what she wants.

From this fact, we can see why men and women are misfiring most of the time. We have two totally different objectives.

THE POWER OF AGREEMENT

In Old Testament days, the prophet Amos asked this important question: *"Can two walk together, except they be agreed?"* (Amos 3:3).

Today, this issue needs to be addressed more than ever.

The word *agreed* in Hebrew means to meet someone at an appointed time. How can a couple journey together unless they see eye to eye on being in the same place at the same time?"

Our culture has so subliminally and directly indoctrinated us to these two polar opposite perspectives that even women who desperately

118

pray for a decent man will choose a dog. Because of her brainwashing, she will look at a man who is celibate and respectful as a weird freak. She will pray for a clean and godly man, and when one shows up, she finds herself not attracted to him—and doesn't know why.

Women have been conditioned to be drawn to bad boys and don't even realize it.

This confusion is accomplished by the media constantly showing images of promiscuous men as being cool, good looking, successful, smooth and the one to be with.

The dominant male society has mastered preconditioning the woman (through movies, print, home training, music, etc.) to view certain behavior as acceptable for men and unacceptable for women. The game necessitates that there be a different set of rules for each sex.

Somehow, many are attracted to a man who has been around the block a few times. For some, it would not be a turn-on if a man were to be inexperienced. At the same time, the person she is drawn to is the perfect candidate to cheat on her and leave her in tears.

Sad but true, she covets what she sees on the album covers, in the romance novels, and who she sees starring in the movies. She wants the exact kind of man that can't commit.

Today's women are not stupid by any means; they are trained by the dominant male culture to view this type of male figure as appealing. This is how sexually exploitive men continue to run the game on every generation of women.

A woman has to reconcile her real needs in a man versus the superficial images that our world has convinced her are worth her time.

Our media-driven culture has intentionally promoted the suggestion of a cool and charismatic character as the ultimate candidate for the woman's affections. The reality is that a woman does not need a cool guy; she needs a godly guy. She doesn't need a pretty boy; she needs a man who will have eyes only for her. She doesn't need an actor out of the movies; rather, a man to live in the real world, faithfully, with her.

There's a vast difference between what she needs versus what she typically wants.

The great deception is that in the woman's heart, she knows that she needs character and integrity in a future spouse, but, in her mind, she has all of these superficial messages that dominate her sensual impulses.

The experienced man knows how to manipulate the woman's internal conflict.

A slick womanizer will know how to play the role of a faithful and godly man, while at the same time projecting those superficial qualities that keep him attractive to the woman on the surface. He will deliver such an Oscar-award-winning performance that the woman will prematurely consider him to be "The One" and begin to give him husband privileges before she even really knows him.

It is wise to make certain that you are both on the same page. Never assume a man really wants what you want. He may very well be just another actor playing a role in one more movie.

THE HUNT

Also, it is common for women to actually discover that a man has been leading them on, but because they are so heavily invested, they pray for the man to grow up and catch up commitment-wise. It's a big mistake to risk that he eventually will get on the same page with you sometime in the future.

The harsh but true reality for a single woman dating a man today is that, in most cases, it mirrors the sport of deer hunting. The man is the hunter and the woman is the prey.

Like every expert hunter, he camouflages his true identity from the target.

The use of camouflage makes the hunted perfectly at ease in a life-threatening situation.

In Old Testament days, the psalmist cried out to God about how wicked men were taking advantage of the poor. The characteristics he illustrated also apply to how a carnal man takes advantage of an unsuspecting woman: *"His mouth is full of cursing and deceit and fraud: under his tongue is mischief and vanity. He sitteth in the lurking places of the villages: in the secret places doth he murder the innocent: his eyes are privily set against the poor. He lieth in wait secretly as a lion in his den: he lieth in wait to catch the poor: he doth catch the poor, when he draweth him into his net"* (Psalms 10:7-9).

The point of these verses is that one group is taking advantage of another. It is a comparison to how society has positioned the woman for manipulation.

Far too often, a female is like a chicken trapped in a field of foxes, unaware. Relative to men, she is at a physical and emotional disadvantage. They are usually promoting a false image that the woman is socially conditioned to believe. But if she accepts the lie it could cost her everything.

I am often accused by my daughters of being too pessimistic when it comes to the trustworthiness of men. This negative viewpoint originates, in part, from my earlier personal experiences in misleading the emotions of women and taking advantage of them.

For my daughters' sake, I would rather be guilty of pessimism and awaken them to consciousness than to be silent and see them broken by deception.

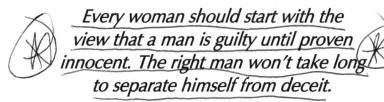

Every woman should start with the view that a man is guilty until proven innocent. The right man won't take long to separate himself from deceit.

CHAPTER 10

MOST MEN ARE ACTORS, SIMPLY PLAYING A ROLE

I cannot emphasize this enough.

Most men are not who they say they are or appear to be. Those who are authentic are few and far between. This is true for a myriad of reasons.

Some men feel a sense of inferiority and presume a need to inflate their profile to create a false measure of security. Others have flaws they attempt to mask with a fake image. Some simply feel the need to manufacture a persona they desire, but, for whatever reason, they have not attained.

On a more diabolical level, a man will assume a false identity for the purpose of deceiving a woman. The deception is aimed at compromising

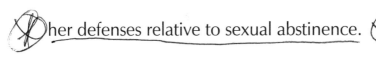 her defenses relative to sexual abstinence.

A man will become anything a woman needs him to be in order to go to bed with her.

The first few faces that a woman sees of a man are not usually genuine. They are characteristics that he knows will appeal to that particular woman, based on data that he quietly and intentionally gathers, for the purpose of manipulating and controlling her emotions.

This dishonesty is not new. King Solomon wrote, *"Most men will proclaim everyone his own goodness: but a faithful man who can find?"* (Proverbs 20:6).

The initial conversation a young woman will have with a man will be laced with a series of half-truths and blatant, prolific prevarication. A man is the master of lying and trickery. When he wants something, he will put on quite a performance.

As a young man growing up in the church and the Pastor's Kid, I became quite an expert at deceit. I played on the fact that I was the minister's son. I spoke very respectfully and was polite to families. I came across as the perfect young man for anyone's daughter.

The entire time, I had a hidden agenda to

125

compromise these young women into a sexual tryst, and I succeeded far too often. I was successful because I sold the young ladies and their families an image that was simply a facade. I was the personification of a wolf in sheep's clothing.

The Bible aptly described me, but I didn't want to listen: *"Beware of false prophets, which come to you in sheep's clothing, but inwardly they are ravening wolves"* (Matthew 7:15).

The evidence of my deceit is revealed in the fact that I was a teenage father before I was sixteen. I had more sexual encounters than I am comfortable sharing, and all of this was unfortunately accomplished by playing roles that young women wanted to see. They fell in love with the image before verifying its authenticity.

Never define a man until you've tested his character.

The reason date rape is possible is because a man has played a role that appealed to a woman's emotions. She lowers her guard down because she trusts the character and then she's blind-sided with sexual assault and, in the worst case scenario, death.

 COMMON CHARACTERS

On the next few pages, I'd like to expose a few common characters that men create to dull the sense of discernment and caution in the opposite sex.

The "Church Guy"

Obviously, this is a person who hangs around church and manipulates the emotions of women who are praying for a biblical husband. This guy will be in the sanctuary every Sunday and even go to Bible study. He aims to paint a portrait of piety and godliness.

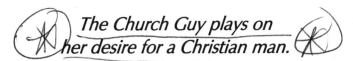

The Church Guy plays on her desire for a Christian man.

He will be the perfect spiritual mate just long enough to get the sister to become vulnerable to his smooth talk. He will accompany her to revival meeting and then ask to have a word of prayer—in her house or apartment. Perhaps that prayer will lead to discussions about how God showed him that she is to be his wife.

Before you know it she is crying tears of joy because she just prayed for God to show her a sign. She leaps up to hug him and he hugs her back.

The next thing you know the sun is coming up and the prayers have turned to repentance.

The tragic reality of the Church Guy's deception is that once he sleeps with the unsuspecting woman, he may disappear from her life and the church. He is a heartless dude.

The "Baller"

This is the fellow who usually drives a nice car and brags about how much money he makes. His specialty is fancy restaurants, and maybe, gifts—if he desires her bad enough. He plays the role to convince the gullible young woman that he will be a great catch that can provide the best things in life.

The baller may even find the money to pay a few of her bills. Once he rescues the young woman from some financial hardship, or spoils her, he moves in for the payoff.

> *The "Baller" guy preys on beautiful women who may be struggling financially.*

The conversation may go something like this: "Let me take you away from all of this pressure and stress. You deserve the best. I want to treat you like a queen. You are the woman I've been praying and hoping for."

He will continue to pour it on until she has some emotional response to his antics. He will use his money to trap the woman into a web of obligation which will lead to her giving in to his sexual advances.

This type of man buys women because he does not plan on settling down with any of them. When he finds someone more appealing or interesting, he (and his wallet) fades off into the sunset.

"Captain Kid"

This individual observes the obvious fact that a woman has children. He likes what he sees, so he uses the kids as a fast track to the bedroom. He targets grocery stores, nursery schools, and any other venue where single moms may frequent. He is probably the lowest of them all. He will use small dogs in the park or other people's babies to cast the impression that he is nurturing and caring.

"Captain Kid" takes an interest in how beautiful, handsome, or smart your child is. He befriends the boy or girl—usually having a lollipop or other types of candy ready to hand them.

Once he wins the child's heart and behaves like the ideal surrogate father for a while, this obliterates the young mother's sense of judgment.

She is so enamored by how he affects her child, she wants to believe it is for real.

Obviously, this guy has learned the fastest lane to the bedroom. Nothing moves a woman like people who love her kids, especially when it is a man and their own father doesn't even react this way.

She gives him any and everything he asks for because she does not want him to leave her kid's life.

Then, one day, out of the blue, he finds a reason to break it off.

Of all of the characters I have described, this guy is the most dangerous because he doesn't only break your heart, he will also hurt your children emotionally. He will do all the right things, and once he gets what he wants, will bail—with no regard for how the children feel about losing a father figure.

It takes time to prove character. A woman should always take the slow track in relationships.

Never become a desperate woman. Be God-fearing and discerning!

CHAPTER 11

THREE STEPS TO HOW A MAN DECEIVES A WOMAN

As I have observed it, in school, church, and life in general, most of the time women are smarter than men. If you were to expose a male and female of equal intelligence to the same task, the woman will usually master the undertaking faster and more completely, barring it is not based purely on physical strength. This raises the question:

How do men get such an upper hand on women?

The answer is simple; women talk too much! A man uses the woman's most common trait against her—he just lets her talk.

R. C. BLAKES, JR.

In the process, the man learns details about the woman's desires, fears, dreams, passions, weaknesses and/or strengths, just by creating an environment for her to share her innermost thoughts.

The main use of the dating concept is to get to know about one another. However, too often the man uncovers what he needs to know to manipulate the woman while she learns nothing about him. Why? Because she did all the talking!

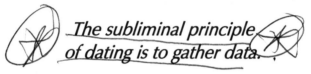

The subliminal principle of dating is to gather data.

Most women are so loose with facts and details that a man does not even need to physically meet them before discovering what they like, don't like and what they hope for in a potential mate.

A man can drill deep into a woman's mind by simply finding her on Facebook. We have all seen it, the lady who gives out too much information just in her profile name. For example: "**Mary** really wants a Christian man who will go to church and tell her how much he loves her."

Upon reading that, he browses through pictures and old posts to figure out what church she goes to, and then the games begin.

In online social media, there are women who tweet everything they are feeling or going through.

Why would a person express their intimate feelings to potentially millions of people who don't matter or care? It is emotional suicide.

Keep your private thoughts to yourself and/or share them only with the people who really love you.

 The object of the game is to press all the buttons that will elevate a woman's emotions and to numb her capacity to think.

THE THREE PHASES

As I learned the game from the older men in my life, there were basically three phases communicated. Allow me to share them with you:

Phase 1: He penetrates the woman's defenses through calculated conversation.

When a man does talk, he is using the power of his words to position the woman into a place of compromise. A wise lady (young or old) pays very close attention to a person who always seems to know what to say. He could be dangerous. As the Bible warns, *"A man that flattereth his neighbor spreadeth a net for his feet"* (Proverbs 29:5).

Flattery is a major cause of foolish decisions. When a man is constantly talking about what you want to hear, be careful.

Women are moved by the right words at the right time.

I have bought my wife jewelry, furs, clothes, shoes, and houses. But in all the years we have been married, I can remember her crying only once when I presented her with a special gift. *The tears flowed when she read what I had written on a card.*

My words touched her in a way that all the gifts never did.

I had the proper motives, but there are some men who don't.

A woman manipulates a man with her body because he's moved by the physical; a man manipulates a woman with words because she is emotional.

Let's take a close look at how Satan, in the Garden of Eden, exposes the woman's vulnerability to words:

134

Now the serpent was more subtle than any beast of the field which the Lord God had made. And he said unto the woman, Yea, hath God said, Ye shall not eat of every tree of the garden?

And the woman said unto the serpent, We may eat of the fruit of the trees of the garden: But of the fruit of the tree which is in the midst of the garden, God hath said, Ye shall not eat of it, neither shall ye touch it, lest ye die.

And the serpent said unto the woman, Ye shall not surely die: for God doth know that in the day ye eat thereof, then your eyes shall be opened, and ye shall be as gods, knowing good and evil.

And when the woman saw that the tree was good for food, and that it was pleasant to the eyes, and a tree to be desired to make one wise, she took of the fruit thereof, and did eat, and gave also unto her husband with her; and he did eat (Genesis 3:1-6).

The Bible calls the serpent "subtle." It means he was crafty and shrewd. This characterizes the clever man who sweet-talks a woman.

As we look at the subliminal messages that

Satan sent to Eve we also see how the man makes a woman view things in a way that serves his evil purposes.

The devil caused Eve to doubt the principles God established. He told her, "I know something that can give you more security." He was implying, "I have your best interest at heart."

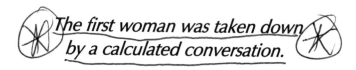

The first woman was taken down by a calculated conversation.

One of the most dangerous things a woman can do with certain men is to open her heart and talk candidly to them. After enticing the woman to reveal her hopes, preferences, and more, he acts like he will be the fulfillment of all her dreams.

Unfortunately, many women become excited about a relationship and share too much too soon. They expose themselves before they know who they are dealing with. You can only learn and discern to the extent you listen. Remember, *"A fool uttereth all his mind: but a wise man keepeth it in till afterwards"* (Proverbs 29:11).

Reserve your deepest and most intimate thoughts until after a man has earned the right to know your heart.

A woman should never entertain a man who allows her to do all of the talking; at best it's a sign of poor leadership skills, on his part, but at worst it is a set-up.

Phase 2: The man works to become the woman's emotional addiction.

Like a predator, a man can be very patient. He paints the picture that he is interested for the long term. This is to create an emotional attachment from the woman to him.

Addictions are created through over-indulgence.

The process is very calculated and deliberate. It goes in a systematic order.

First: He overdoses her on time spent.

To a woman, when a man gives of his time, it means that he is interested in her. Too often the reality is that he is only paying attention because of what he wants from her. Once he's reached his hidden desire, he often moves on.

How often do we hear women complain, "When we first got together, he gave me all of his time; now I get none"? The first sign of a man retreating is when a woman has to beg for his attention.

Second: He overdoses her on flattery.

The way to an inexperienced woman's heart is through kind words, even if they are not sincere.

When the Old Testament prophet Daniel was recording the prophecy of the Antichrist, he wrote that he will be a flatterer. As it is written, *"And such as do wickedly against the covenant shall he corrupt by flatteries: but the people that do know their God shall be strong, and do exploits"* (Daniel 11:32).

The spirit of the Antichrist comes to deceive, destroy, and pervert God's people.

> ### The key ingredient
> ### to deception is flattery.

Just as a man loses all sense of judgment when a woman flaunts her body, a woman is disarmed just as quickly by a man who showers her with compliments.

Third: He overdoses her with romance.

Romance is the process of a man doing everything he knows a woman will respond to in order to prepare her for a sexual encounter. He will buy flowers, candy, and cards. He will wine and dine her and go to extravagant levels to stir up the woman's sexual attraction toward him.

There is a biblical record of how an unfaithful wife seduced a gullible man. Although the text paints the woman as a harlot, it exposes the tactics of any emotional predator. She said all of the right words, wore the right clothes, set the atmosphere, and broke his will: *"With her much fair speech she caused him to yield, with the flattering of her lips she forced him. He goeth after her straightway, as an ox goeth to the slaughter, or as a fool to the correction of the stocks; Till a dart strike through his liver; as a bird hasteth to the snare, and knoweth not that it is for his life"* (Proverbs 7:21-23)

Just as this woman controlled this unsuspecting man, females today, to a large degree, are captured and managed like an inanimate object. She is placed into a sexual situation before she realizes what is really happening.

> ***Once she submits to sex, she's exposed to everything and the dynamics become much more complicated.***

When a woman is finally enticed sexually, she

becomes one with the man—physically, emotionally, and spiritually. This partner, and everyone he's been with, now has access to her life. Remember, Scripture tells us, *"Know ye not that he which is joined to a harlot is one body? for two, saith he, shall be one flesh"* (1 Corinthians 6:16).

Though this text talks about a female predator, the reverse is true. When a woman is beguiled by the advances of a manipulative man, she is joined to him. She will be impacted by that decision in practically every phase of her life from that point on.

Phase 3: He avoids making a real commitment.

There are men who will happily hang around as long as the woman is satisfied being classified as his girlfriend. Once the conversation turns serious, he squirms and becomes uneasy. His actions mirror this verse: *"Confidence in an unfaithful man in time of trouble is like a broken tooth, and a foot out of joint"* (Proverbs 25:19).

A man can make more excuses for avoiding commitment than a criminal makes to stay out of jail. A wise woman will test a suitor's faithfulness prior to fully investing herself into the union.

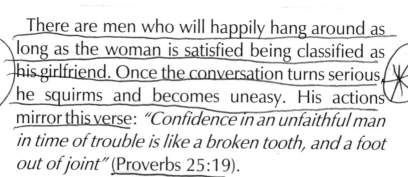

An ungodly, unfaithful man can stoop to what I consider record lows to back out of a relationship. He will blame it on a lack of finances, and even chastise God for not giving him clarity. The truth is, he just does not want to commit.

The most sickening of tactics is when a man plays a psychological game, making the woman feel that something is wrong with her. His excuses will run the gamut from, "She's not tidy enough around the house," to "I don't think she is supportive of my dreams."

He will create random arguments. All of this is to detract from the subject of commitment.

He then fabricates a bogus
reason to cut the cord and dump her.

To avoid endless years of heartache, take the time to understand his deception.

141

CHAPTER 12

RELATIONSHIP GAMES AND HOW THEY'RE PLAYED

W hile I was in the process of writing *The Father-Daughter Talk*, it came to me; there are common everyday games that depict the emotional sport that men have made of dating.

Some of the schoolyard and board games that children innocently play may have subliminally influenced how men think about their relationships with women.

In my office, as I worked on this book, my assistant came in for a second. We enjoyed looking at the similarities between a few popular childhood activities and the games grown men play.

RELATIONSHIP GAMES

MONKEY BARS

When I was a child at Lafayette Elementary School in New Orleans, I loved to play on the Monkey Bars.

It was a configuration of bars, elevated off the ground. Each bar was laid out, one in front of the other, about eight to twelve inches apart. The idea of the game was for the child to swing from one bar to the next in any direction of the child's choosing. You could swing forward, sideways or backwards.

Based on the concept of this schoolyard activity, we can see the same principles applied to how certain men mismanage their relationships with women.

When a guy constantly acts like he's letting go and doesn't want the relationship one moment, then calls the next as if nothing happened, he is playing Monkey Bars.

He swings backwards and forwards, in and out, and up and down. This leaves the woman in a state of confusion, hanging in limbo, emotionally paralyzed, and not able to move on. This is intentional on the man's part. It is his way of

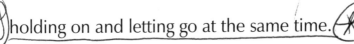

holding on and letting go at the same time.

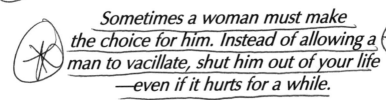

Sometimes a woman must make the choice for him. Instead of allowing a man to vacillate, shut him out of your life —even if it hurts for a while.

I tried to play this very game with my wife Lisa, when we were dating. I had a serious commitment phobia. I knew that I loved Lisa and she was the one for me; however, I did not want the obligation of being exclusive, yet I didn't like the thought of her being with another man.

I would continually create planned chaos. I would find a reason to be angry and uncertain about our future. This would lead to abruptly ending phone calls and indirectly calling our relationship off.

A day or so would pass and I would surface again. I would never allow enough time to lapse so that she could actually adjust to my absence and move on. I liked being able to swing back and forth. It was the dating equivalent of having one's cake and eating it too.

As time went on, I became bolder and bolder with my antics. I would almost schedule the episodes based on previous plans. One day I swung too far to recover and it all fell apart. I said, "I don't want to get married. It would be best if you just moved on."

I had never gone so far as to emphatically declare a hard position. Lisa simply replied, "Okay," and hung up.

Because I had taken such a stern stance, I didn't know how to undo this mistake.

Lisa moved on and began dating a professional athlete. Obviously, I had swung too far this time.

One day, my mother was talking to me about how my life was going, and some of the errors I was making. At the top of her list was the fact that I was letting Lisa go. She talked about how I was getting to be too old to continue teenage blunders and needed to build a solid foundation.

She told me to go and get Lisa back, which, thankfully, I did. I called Lisa, put on my best Blakes' charm, and the rest is history. This time, I was sincere.

I may have never made a real decision to commit if Lisa had not been strong enough to let me go.

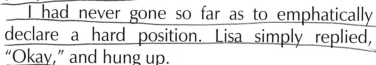

No woman should allow a man to swing in and out of her life.

You are losing your best years to an indecisive individual who may never get it together. It is best to move on than to hang on, only to grow older and bitter.

MERRY-GO-ROUND

This game is probably the schoolyard favorite of children around the world. I loved the merry-go-round when I was a kid. It is a fast and exciting ride that moves around and around in a circle. It gives the participants a fast and exhilarating rush, while they actually go nowhere.

This ride also mimics a certain game that men play with women. They take her on an emotional trip that has no destination. It's a fast-moving approach filled with sex, money, promises of commitment, break ups, and makes ups. Yet they always end where they started, only to repeat the cycle all over again.

The object of this game is to move so fast the woman is constantly off balance. By the time they are through spinning you around, you realize, after many years, you're still in the same place you started.

Let me illustrate this with the testimony of an anonymous woman:

I met a man in college. He appeared to be everything a young woman could dream of. He had money, though I had no clue as to where it came from. He drove fast cars,

146

bought expensive gifts and was a passionate lover.

My young mind was so blown it was twenty years later that I realized this man was never going to marry me and had moved me so fast that I forsook the values of my faith and the wishes of my parents.

After three kids out of wedlock and me being in the midlife stage, he left me for a younger woman. At first, our relationship felt right, but I was badly mistaken.

The Bible does tell us that "there are ways that seem correct, but end in destruction."

I should have slowed things down and payed more attention.

A man who has good intentions will move fast enough for a woman to know he's serious and slow enough for her to see the progress. She will be comfortable with his moves.

TWISTER

This is a game that is played on the floor. It has a mat with various colored circles. Multiple people participate and spin a wheel to determine where the next move should be made. Whatever color the arrow stops on, a foot or hand has to be placed on that color. The players get so *twisted up* that they can't see where one starts and the other ends.

This, too, describes certain games that men play.

The man will twist the woman up into an emotional ball of confusion with random acts of calculated kindness until she is lost in him.

He will make financial contributions to obligate her. Then he will invite the woman to meet his family and cut her off from her friends.

The man will occupy her every waking moment—all of which is designed to twist the woman's identity into one that is shared with him. He does not want her to be able to stand alone apart from him.

The woman will eventually lose her identity and be totally controlled.

I was watching a popular daytime talk show that featured two educated women who were living in a house with one man. They, against their will, shared this one guy sexually. They hated each other, but they shared a man.

Some of their reasons for not leaving were: "He's kind, caring, polite, and the father of our children."

They both were hoping that he would make a decision for one or the other. It was quite obvious that he had no intention of making any such choice when he remarked, "I think they both belong to me."

Finally, the host got the man to admit that he was operating a system to control these women. It was apparent that he had psychologically and emotionally subjugated them and they appeared to have no will of their own.

He had twisted them into a mass of confusion, obligation, and manipulation. They didn't know which way to turn.

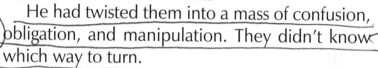

Never let a man tie your life down until he has lovingly placed a ring on your finger.

It is never a good idea to have babies with a man you're not married to—and you shouldn't live with a man who is not your husband. It's an unhealthy arrangement.

SORRY

The object of the board game, "Sorry," is to get one's entire set of pieces safely home. On the journey, there are other players who are trying to reach home as well. When the opponents encounter each other on the board, they bump each other back to square one. When they do this, they always have to say, "Sorry."

This speaks for itself. There will be men who do

149

you no good because they have no goodness within them. Their sole purpose is to selfishly have their way with a woman and to string her along with a never ending series of apologies.

This represents the brother who serves no purpose in a woman's life other than to continuously knock her backwards and, in the process, have fits of remorse.

He adds nothing and subtracts from every part of her life, yet all he ever says is,"I'M SORRY!"

This individual can cry at the drop of a hat. He will dominate the conversation with emotional expressions that could bring tears to the eyes of a police officer. He's smart—like a street psychologist who gets into your head.

At some point the woman should demand more than him on one knee, with tears and screams of pseudo remorse. Be sure there are definite signs that he is really changing for the better.

ROLLER COASTER

This is a theme park favorite. The roller coaster is a main attraction with its twisted turns and rising and falling rails. It's a thrill ride designed to give one the experience of great highs and sudden lows. The riders never have a secure sense of being. Everything about it creates instability.

The roller coaster guy sells the woman many thrilling dreams and pie-in-the-sky hopes that go nowhere.

The relationship fluctuates from extremely hopeful to depressingly uncertain. It's rarely a consistent and steady flow; instead, its bipolar.

This guy is usually big on drinking and drugs. He excites the woman because he's fast moving and unpredictable. He stirs a certain aspect of the woman's interest as he skates around her greater needs. He keeps the ride going so fast that there is rarely a settled moment to address the woman's real longterm dreams.

Eventually she finds herself drained emotionally and broken psychologically. She hits a wall of depression because she realizes that this ride is going nowhere.

Every woman should understand that one of the greatest attributes in a man is stability and dedication. Fast rides can be dangerous—and expensive!

A FINAL WORD

It is my prayer that you have been empowered by what you have read on these pages.

Take a moment to review the 12 principles we have discussed and apply them to your personal life.

1. Your Dress Code Is Your Personal Commercial

Believe me when I tell you that how you dress has more to do with your public, professional, and relational perception than you realize. You, as a woman, must dress intentionally.

Don't promote the stereotype of womanhood being purely for sexual stimulation and gratification. There is nothing more socially disrespectful than to be looked upon as a physical utensil for men to use. Never provoke ignorance towards women by the way you present yourself to the world.

2. Your Value Is Not Determined By a Relationship With A Man

It is imperative that you receive this message.

Multitudes of women are in torment because they have not attained certain levels of relationships with men. Society has so fractured the woman's sense of individuality that she sees herself as incomplete and/or defective in the absence of a male bond that is meaningful.

The problem arises when her desire is bent more towards "a relationship" than the "right relationship." She often finds her value in this and settles for people who are beneath her.

Know your worth as a stand-alone person.

3. Never Lay Your Body Down for a Man Who Has Not Laid His Life Down for You

This speaks of reserving sex until a man has put a ring on your finger. Never give your body to one who doesn't make a lifelong commitment.

> *Commitment is a synonym for manhood. A man that can't commit is not worthy of your greatest gift*

4. Never Be With A Man Who Makes You Afraid

The first thing a woman should get from a man is a sense of security. Any male who is perceived to be a threat is automatically disqualified. A true man would never give his woman any sign that he could remotely become physically aggressive with her.

As a woman you must establish your non-negotiable rules and non-violence should be at the top of the list. A woman has to resist the first signs of abuse and sever that relationship immediately.

When violence is an issue there is no exit strategy necessary. She should flee such a relationship like people evacuate a burning building; get out by means of the first exit available. Jump out of the window if you must. Just get out!

Never fall into the trap of thinking that you can change a man who is an abuser.

A person who uses physical force is broken and his victim is certainly not the person to fix him. Would an emergency room doctor treat an individual who brutally attacked him in the alley? No. That would be a job for someone else.

5. A Woman Must Be Prepared to Earn Her Own Money

The one thing she must do for herself is to make herself employable—and ultimately an employer. In other words, powerful women can handle financial matters. This is the wrong era for a female to put her financial hopes on the shoulders of a man.

There are a few things to consider if a woman is expecting a man to be her financial savior. First, she must ask herself, "Will I actually have a man to take care of me?" Second, "Will he make enough money to really provide and secure a future?"

The third thing to ponder should be, "If I do have a husband who can provide, what happens to me if he dies prematurely?"

 My father always said "It is better to have and not need than to need and not have."

6. Most Men Will Say Anything For Sex

Every woman must suspect that a man is saying whatever it takes to compromise her sexually.

The fastest way to separate a man who is playing games from a serious contender is to establish boundaries pertaining to sex

The mindset of many women, is to give in sexually, believing that it will draw the man closer. In reality, sex actually pushes the man farther away. Once he has the ultimate experience with your body he may find a reason to rid himself of you before marriage. Please don't forget this!

155

7. When A Man Has a Woman's Body He Has Her Soul

Soul ties are real. They are a connection to another person that won't allow them to move forward independently.

When you give your body to a man, you are allowing him access to your whole being. It is not just a physical act; it is an emotional, psychological, and spiritual impartation.

A woman's first lover, if not her husband, may haunt her sex life forever. She will, in some cases, be ill prepared to enjoy the man that God gave to her in covenant. In the back of her mind there may remain continuous thoughts of her first lover.

8. A Man Will Always Settle With the Woman He Respects

Ladies, please resist the temptation to give a man everything he wants before its time. While you are thinking that you're using an irresistible strategy, he is viewing your liberality as a character flaw. He may be more attracted to you; but, he will ultimately settle down with the woman that had certain boundaries and enforced them.

If a woman is too easy sexually, he will then expand on that label and see her as an easy target for any man.

Demand respect and never settle for anything less.

9. Understand the Games Men Play

The basis of the game starts with the man deceiving the woman. She expects commitment while he does everything he can to avoid it.

The game is to make the woman believe she is on the same page when they are actually reading from different books.

10. Most Men are Actors Playing a Role

In his aim to deceive the woman, a man plays various roles. If she's a church-going lady he will play the "Church Dude." If she has kids, he will play the role of "Captain Kid." If the woman is financially needy he will play the part of "The Baller."

The point is, the woman must never take the first face of a man as being authentic. Give the process time to uncover the real person.

11. Three Steps to How the Man Deceives the Woman

I have discovered that the process a deceptive

157

man will take to circumvent the woman's better judgement is generally in three stages.

The first is to break down her defenses through calculated conversation that appeals to her personality.

The second stage moves into becoming the woman's emotional addiction. He carefully does this through overdosing her on all of the things that she likes.

The third stage is to avoid commitment at all cost.

12. Relationship Games and How They're Played

The games men seem to enjoy can be compared to board and schoolyard games.

Some men will play the "Monkey Bars" game. He will swing in and out of a woman's life while holding on at the same time.

Others put you on a "Merry-Go-Round"—a fast trip with no real destination. You may also play "Twister," which results in so much confusion that you lose your identity. Then there's "Sorry"—with plenty of apologies, yet no real change.

Finally, you find yourself on a "Roller Coaster," with highs and lows that leave you drained emotionally.

GOD HAS A WONDERFUL FUTURE PREPARED FOR YOU

I have embraced this subject and shared these principles with sincerity, passion, and dedication. It is my prayer that you, as a woman, will apply the teachings of this book so that the playing field will become level and the man God has chosen for you will come into your life.

Please share these truths with as many young women as possible. It can save them from unnecessary turmoil and lead them into the marvelous future the Lord has planned.

FOR ADDITIONAL RESOURCES OR TO
SCHEDULE THE AUTHOR FOR SPEAKING
ENGAGEMENTS, CONTACT:

R. C. BLAKES, JR. MINISTRIES
P.O. BOX 571083
HOUSTON, TX 77257

PHONE: 504-569-8205
WEBSITE: www.rcblakes.com
EMAIL: fatherdaughtertalk@gmail.com